MEDIA AND SOCIETY

By the same Author

Handbook of Journalism and Mass Communication with **Prof. V.S. Gupta**

Translation of two AMIC publications (in Hindi) with **Prof. V.S. Gupta**

— *Press Systems in SAARC* and

— *Role of Media in National Crisis*

About the Editor

Vir Bala Aggarwal, a senior researcher and academic, had a brilliant scholastic career in MJ and B. Tech (Printing Technology). She worked on role of mass media in development, for her dissertation for Ph.D.

She has published and presented a large number of papers on media issues in journals and regional and national seminars. Presently working as the Chairperson, Department of Journalism and Mass Communication, Himachal Pradesh University, Shimla. She specialises in communication theory, printing technology and development issues; and is associated with a number of journalism departments as a resource person.

MEDIA AND SOCIETY
CHALLENGES AND OPPORTUNITIES

Edited by
VIR BALA AGGARWAL
Chairperson,
Department of Journalism
and Mass Communication,
Himachal Pradesh University
Shimla

CONCEPT PUBLISHING COMPANY, NEW DELHI-110059

ISBN : 81-7022-996-0

First Published 2002

Published and Printed by
Ashok Kumar Mittal
Concept Publishing Company
A/15-16, Commercial Block, Mohan Garden,
New Delhi-110059

Phones : 5351460, 5351794
Fax : 091-11-5357103
E-mail : publishing@conceptpub.com

FOREWORD

India, with over one billion population, is a plural and multilingual society. It has a wide range of communication media, extending from interpersonal methods of communication to satellite broadcasting, from a two-page broad sheet in a regional language printed on a treadle so common in small towns and villages even now, to multi-edition dailies through facsimile printing process, the second largest broadcasting service in the world, an expanding television and cable TV system and now the emerging multimedia and internet revolution. The newspapers in India are published in nearly 100 languages. Internet editions of newspapers are coming up quite fast. Keeping pace with the contemporary trends, the media is progressively becoming market-driven and technology oriented. The term mass media itself has become greatly enlarged and now there is an ongoing debate on knowledge *vs.* skills, method *vs.* medium, and theory *vs.* praxis.

And these days, the information super-highways are bridging not only peoples and cultures or countries and communities but also hopes and aspirations. Media is acting as a vehicle of education and extension; an instrument of social change and social justice; a watchdog and a social corrective. Because of its reach and impact, it is sensitizing people about the crucial role they can play in stepping up the pace of economic development and nation building. It is also contributing to political image building and indoctrination. Yet it is against *status quo*. It has been serving both tradition and modernity; continuity and change; historical processes and contemporary situations, and analysing and projecting linkages between idea and event and patterns of social change and directions of policy. The compulsions of market forces to which it has too willy-nilly to submit, of course, are increasingly circumscribing all this, Media is no longer regarded as a mission but a commercial venture and a professional pursuit.

It is, therefore, gratifying to note that these and varied other themes affecting society and media were discussed in three separate sessions on contemporary media landscape; media and development; and media policy issues at the Seminar hosted by the Department of Journalism and Mass Communication of our University in October 2000.

The Department has made good progress: MJMC programme has been introduced in the Department; its lab journal has been revived, and a number of eminent media experts have been invited for interaction.

I place on record my appreciation for the hard work put in by the Chairperson of the Department, Dr. (Mrs.) Vir Bala Aggarwal, her colleagues and students in organising a successful seminar. I also congratulate her on bringing out this publication—*Media and Society : Challenges and Opportunities* which has partly grown out of the papers presented at the seminar. I am sure, this will go a long way in disseminating knowledge about the latest trends in media development.

I also extend my best wishes for the success of this publication and hope that the commendable efforts put in by Dr. (Mrs.) Aggarwal will be continued in future for the development of the discipline and the Department.

S.K. Gupta
Vice-Chancellor
Himachal Pradesh University

ACKNOWLEDGEMENTS

This book has grown out of the papers presented at Seminar on 'Media and Society : Challenges and Opportunities' held at Himachal Pradesh University, Shimla by Department of Journalism and Mass Communication on 23-24 October, 2000. It was a long standing professional urge to discover and report on what media had been doing for this country. A large number of distinguished scholars from all over the country, several of them with lifetime devotion to profession, faculty members from Universities and media professionals participated in the seminar. An effort has been made to produce the views of all those who participated and also of other media academics.

The author acknowledges all those professionals who have tried their best to update and revise their chapters to reflect the tremendous changes that have occurred in mass media in recent years.

I wish to place on record my sincere gratitude to :—

1. Late Prof. S.K. Gupta, Vice-Chancellor of Himachal Pradesh University, Shimla, who encouraged and helped in several ways in organising the Seminar, based on which the publication is being brought out;
2. Prof. V.S. Gupta, former professor, Haryana Agricultural University, Hissar who guided and motivated me to complete the work in time;
3. Mr. Ashok Mittal, the publisher for his keen cooperation and interest in bringing out this publication; and
4. Finally, I wish to thank all of the faculty members and students who supported me at every step of the seminar.

1st October, 2001 **Vir Bala Aggarwal**

CONTENTS

INTRODUCTION

VIR BALA AGGARWAL

The National Seminar on "Media and Society : Challenges and Opportunities", organized by the Department of Journalism and Mass Communication, Himachal Pradesh University on 23-24 October 2000 elicited a large number of papers on contemporary media landscape including Online Journalism, dot.com Journalism, Critical Review of the IT Act and Mass Media Technology, Regional Press and the current Print Media-Scenario in the country. The quality of papers and interest shown in the convergence of communication technology shows that media educators are bracing themselves to face the challenges of new communication technology.

Some of the eminent media professionals attending the Seminar were : Mr. Shyam Khosla, Veteran Journalist and President-elect, National Union of Journalists who also delivered the keynote address; Mr. Radhye Shyam Sharma, Editorial Advisor, *Dainik Bhaskar,* Chandigarh; Mr. Prem Kumar, former Resident Editor, *Indian Express,* Chandigarh; Prof. M.R. Dua, former Professor, IIMC; and Prof. B.K. Kuthiala, GJU, Hissar. Mr. Justice Om Prakash, Lokayukta and Chairman, Human Rights Commission, Himachal Pradesh inaugurated the Seminar and Mr. Vishnu Kant Shastri, Governor of Himachal Pradesh delivered the Valedictory Address. The Vice-Chancellor, Prof. S.K. Gupta presided over the functions on both the days. The seminar organized by the Department for the first time in 14 years ever since its inception in 1986 was convened and conducted by the Chairperson, Dr. (Mrs.) Vir Bala Aggarwal.

Inagurating the Seminar, the Chairperson of the Himachal Pradesh Human Rights Commission, Mr. Justice Om Prakash, decried the tendency of the media to play up sensitive cases during the period of trial and said Court reporting should not be done till the final judgement is announced. He observed that media has emerged as the strongest pillar of domocracy in the country and mediapersons should contribute to shaping the society and try to restore confidence in the rural people by ensuring the flow of desirable information to them. Justice Om Prakash observed that the climate of consumerism created by the electronic media had created unrest amongst the deprived sections of society.

He also released the publication brought out by the Department on the occasion. The publication, besides containing the abstracts of papers presented in the Seminar also included the Directory of the BJMC students who have passed out since the establishment of the Department in 1986.

Summary of the Papers Presented

The thrust of papers presented in the section on contemporary media landscape included the versatility and reach of internet, potential for actual and possible use of computers in various stages of newspaper production and strength and weaknesses of online journalism.

Internet is yet another technological magic toy. It has conquered distances, time and speed. The whole world opens up in its full glory and marvel. Internet is an inexhaustive depository of knowledge and information is available all the 24 hours in any part of the globe. All kinds of information is at the disposal of users on amazing range of subjects.

The process of news collection at the level of reporters and correspondents is also changing. News persons can send information on e-mail. The practice of distributing press releases is also gradually being replaced first by the use of fax and then by e-mail. Moreover, whatever the organization wishes to share with media is available on the websites as and when required.

Perhaps no other factor would qualify for the shrinking of the world into a global village more than the emergence of online journalism cutting across political boundaries, predilections and prejudices. Understanding the emergence of this new form of journalism is vital for its judicious use, both, as an instrument of informational traffic and national development.

The end users can get updated information from this global medium any time, most of the online periodicals being free. Hyperlinks permit choice from a vast ocean of topics and archival facility provides an easy access to the newspaper morgue. Multimedia assists effective communication of the message by way of audio-visual aids. For news persons, online journalism has opened more job avenues and offers wider readership. The management profits from the revenue generated by the advertisements posted online. The popularity chart of a new website is just a click away for the management. Number of hits recorded display the readership status and, thus, offers scope for change in the light of this response. Letters to editors, opinion polls and discussions provide a platform for interaction among various social and professional groups. However, problems like high cost factor, lack of computer literacy, low bandwidth, enormous network traffic and conservative attitude towards new technology can, to a certain extent, decelerate the development of online media. Besides, infringement of copyright, defamation attempts and obscenity that presently go unchecked in the absence of adequate cyber laws could be sources of trouble for the government and the general public.

For the news professionals, online journalism has created more job avenues. A new genre of specialized personnel is emerging in the form of web editors, content providers, web visualizers, web graphic designers, etc. However, this benefit can trickle down to audience only if the intellectuals who wrote for the literati become technology driven computer friendly. The editors have to cater to newer skills and transform the capability of their newsrooms and editorial chambers to make sense out of both the real and virtual worlds.

Notwithstanding the many of the shortcomings attendant on it, online journalism seems to have withstood the test of time reflected as it is in the increasing size of its audience. Besides, it provides a medium where print, audio and video converge and a user-friendly interface satiates the emotional and aesthetics palate of an individual. The ability of web news to cut down the time to get across, to cross the barrier of manual or postal distribution and to bridge the communities separated by geographical boundaries, cannot be overlooked.

The phenomenal expansion of language press, resulting in single daily domination in several States is another salient feature of the contemporary media scenario in the country. The language newspapers closer as they are to the local communities reflect the cultural and literary traditions of the people they serve. The rapid technological developments, which the print media is adapting to survive, has also brought about far reaching changes. Several print media organizations have been developing comprehensive websites of their own, which regularly cover interviews, chat shows, business and economy news, life styles and entertainment. Some of the newspapers which were confined to parts of States like Uttar Pradesh and Madhya Pradesh have not only expanded within those States but have also crossed the State barriers and covered new grounds. They have also kept pace with technology and have been going in for professionalism, both in business and editorial functions in most cases.

Some of the reasons for the fast growth of regional press are : Greater democratization of society creating a desire on the part of the people for information and knowledge; Development of corporate culture resulting in exploration of new audiences for advertisement; Greater competition between print and electronic media leading to improvement in quality of regional press; Advances in technology for printing and communication leading to many statellite editions of newspapers.

Valedictory Address

The Chancellor of the University and Governor of Himachal Pradesh, His Excellency Mr. Vishnu Kant Shastri, who was the chief guest at the valedictory function, in his address expressed concern over commercialisation of media leading to negation of social objectives. This has resulted in improvement in the packaging of news and its superficial presentation, but there has been an overall lack of depth in the treatment of important social issues. The missionary zeal that the media had during the freedom struggle when veteran freedom fighters like Mahatma Gandhi, Lokmanya Tilak and Ganesh Shankar Vidyarthi had challenged the British Government was no longer there.

The Vice-Chancellor, Dr. Gupta announced that the Department would be provided a computer lab and a multimedia lab so as to give training to the students in media technology. An internet connection has already been provided. The Department introduced MJMC classes with effect from the academic session.

KEYNOTE ADDRESS

SHYAM KHOSLA

During the freedom movement, media was perceived to be a mission. Mahatma Gandhi, Lokmanya Tilak, Lajpat Rai and Veer Savarkar used the media to inform and educate the masses and to involve them in the great endeavour to free India from the foreign yoke. After independence, the business houses and the money bags saw in the newspaper industry an opportunity not only to earn money but also to acquire political clout. Media persons too conveniently forgot the mission and looked upon journalism as a profession. There is nothing wrong in this perception if the practitioners of this profession remember that it is not a vehicle to acquire political clout for petty personal ends. It is a profession through which one can earn his livelihood even as one serves the society.

Media and Social Change

Media is not only a mirror of the society but also an instrument of social change. It must inform and educate the society and also act as a medium of communication between various organs of the society, between the government and the masses and between the elected representatives and the voter. Media must have a close look at the society in all its manifestation with a penetrating eye. Its job is to reflect the aspirations of the people and to spread noble ideas. It must expose social evils and help in their eradication. It is its responsibility to critically examine facts and to project them in an objective manner without fear or favour. A journalist is a trustee of the society and must not betray the trust reposed in him.

Credibility is the key word. If a newspaper loses its credibility, it is not worth the paper it is printed on. In this connection, let me recall what Prem Bhatia, a highly respected Editor with whom I had the honour to work with in *The Tribune* said at a seminar organised by the Haryana Union of Journalists. I quote: "A journalist who has sold his soul is no better than a street walker. Unfortunately, our profession has not only street walkers but also call girls namely highly paid editors". This was an expression of deep anguish of a professional journalist at the current state of affairs. There cannot be a more powerful denunciation of the bad fish in the profession that have dragged the media into a morass of commercialism and trivia.

Media and Democracy

Chairman of the Press Council, Justice P.B. Sawant points out that in a democracy, the people are not the subjects or the ruled. They are the rulers with the duty and obligation to govern themselves and govern well. The people have, therefore, to be well informed and equipped to discharge their obligations. It is the media that is in a position to discharge this function effectively. It has a major role to play in preserving and promoting democracy by safeguarding the independence of various institutions of the State and ensuring their accountability. It can play this role only if it is independent and free. That is why the monopoly over the media of the government or of an individual and a private institution is *per se* dangerous and poses a serious threat to the democratic polity.

Media has an important public duty as guardian of democratic values. Freedom of the Press implies freedom from censorship or intimidation from any quarter—big business, political parties, governments or employers. A newspaper is not a piece of property but a living personality with a character and tradition deriving not only from those who own or edit it but also from its readers, the causes it has historically served and the community of which it is a part. It is no secret to those who work in the media or watch its functioning from close quarters that many of the greatest challenges to a free and independent media now come not from governments but from many of the proprietors.

Working Conditions of Journalists

Media is an industry with a social commitment. It is an industry in which information is the product that must be circulated undiluted and objectively. Unfortunately, many a proprietor avail of all the facilities from the Government in the name of running an independent newspaper but use the media to promote his business interests and to acquire political clout. Not only that, the proprietors tend to deprive the journalists of a fair wage. It is my fundamental belief that a free media cannot exist where journalists work in conditions of poverty and insecurity. Strong and independent journalism cannot operate unless journalists feel confident in their employment. That is why the contract system should not apply to journalists. It restricts their freedom. The contract journalists feel insecure about their jobs as they do not know if their fixed time contracts will be renewed or not. This makes them compliant and they lose the freedom to write what they perceive to be true and in the interest of the society. Part time correspondents and photojournalists are the most exploited lot among media persons. In most cases, they are wrongly denied the status of a journalist and reasonably good working conditions. Most of them are denied the wages they are entitled to under the law of the land.

Freelance Journalists

Freelancing is fast emerging as an area of journalistic activity that presents a plethora of serious challenges.

Ironically, job market of regular and secure employment is shrinking even while work opportunities are expanding as never before. Senior journalists are forced to accept short-term contracts or subjected to conditions that are totally unacceptable to those professionals who are unwilling to compromise with their dignity. These freelancers offer their services for hire for production of editorial material by individual arrangements that are often unwritten and uncertain. Unfortunately, their legal status as working journalists is not yet clear. Although a freelance journalist whose principal avocation is journalism is by logic and law a working journalist, a narrow and flawed interpretation of the law prevented the Manisana Wage Board from fixing a minimum rate of remuneration for them. There is a clear case for appropriate amendments to the Working Journalists Act to define the status of freelancers.

Increasingly, employers are using employment arrangements that undermine job security and fair wages. If the employers think that a weak and compliant journalist is good for them, they are wrong. In the long run, journalists who are insecure and underpaid cannot produce the sort of journalism that is essential for a vibrant democratic and creative culture that is so important in the world today.

Eclipse of the Editor

Two significant developments underline the destruction of the institution of editor that was the bulwark against attacks on the freedom and independence of the Press. One is that hard decisions on what to carry and how to carry are no longer taken by the editorial team but by the commercial side on the newspaper establishment. In the license permit *raj* era newspaper owners used the media to protect their business interests but apart from certain opinionated attacks on their political and business rivals, the news selection, display and decisions about whom to assign the story were taken by the editor or his representative. Now, that area of editorial action has shrunk and in certain newspapers, including the mass circulated dailies, it has almost disappeared.

While the *Time* group designates editors as editors of specified markets and not for editions, the *Hindustan Times* has the proprietor herself as the Editorial Director and the *Indian Express* has made its Editor-in-Chief as the CEO of the company. In most regional newspapers, the owners themselves are designated as editors though several of them cannot write a single line barring the appointment and dismissal letters of their employees. The result of the owners masquerading as editors is that the space that their hardworking correspondent should occupy has been usurped from the hacks to be adorned by creepy crows of capitalism preening themselves as peacocks of journalism with a few colourful feathers attached for effect.

It will be interesting to recall an incident when a proprietor of a newspaper nominated himself in a team of science reporters that were taken to Moscow to cover the launching of Commander Rakesh Sharma with Soviet cosmonauts in a Soviet space ship in 1984. He cabled the following story to his paper from Moscow: *Commander Sharma Blasted Into Space. Take Agency. Give My Byline.*

Electronic Media

The sacrifice of hard news at the altar of commercialization is creeping into the media at an alarming speed. Journalists are under tremendous pressure from their proprietors to accommodate commercial news that is no more than commercial publicity material. It is destroying fearless and investigating journalism. TV channels are trying to raise viewers' attendance for news with visuals that could hook them. Television news, wittingly or unwittingly, is contributing to the dumbing down of the society. Under the influence of commercialism, the prime news slot of the Star TV has been shifted from the Star Plus channel. The vacated place has been given to the largest audience rated show in the country *Kaun Banega Crorepati*. Not to be left behind, rival TV channels are launching different shows with ten times the prize money. At this rate, people will be served chicken soup for their souls and never good nourishment for their minds.

Challenges of Convergence

The convergence of media with communication, business and entertainment based on the great revolution in information technology is a challenge and an opportunity. A convergence bill is under preparation. The draft bill shows that the idea is to have a mega regulatory body that will control communication, broadcasting and electronic journalism. A single body will regulate careers and content. There is a serious threat to true information in this. Technocrats, whose vision is proverbially narrow, will sit on judgement over news and views content on the Internet. The ability of one and all to log on to the Internet raises the issues of far deeper consequences to journalism than the censorship of the print media.

As journalists, we will have to deal with the immense power that Internet gives us. Nothing prevents us from starting a web page and generate a newspaper on the web of our own. But there are dangers on the horizon. One is the immense desire of the authorities to control flow of news on the net fearing the power it delivers to the people at all levels. Another is the temptation of mega media owners to buy up successful dot.coms and integrate them into the media empires. Rupert Murdoch's Star TV has a great influence on the Indian middle class and his rival Kerry Packer has got a good foothold in a telecom company that has now branched out into the entertainment world that will not exclude media for long. The pressure is building on the Government to lift the ban on foreign media and the Minister of Information and Broadcasting says the Government has an open mind on the subject. Media and the intellectuals will have to raise their voice against this dangerous move. We can do without foreign media.

In the fast changing scenario of transformation of news into media and media into infotainment, journalists will have to redefine the purpose of their being in the profession. One thing they must do immediately is to master the new technologies. But that will not be enough. We will have to set a moral high ground to ensure that it lives in the hearts of the people and that would mean we educate people to understand and appreciate the significance of news to their daily lives.

Press Council

Press Council is a statutory body set under the Press Council Act of 1978 with the object of preserving the freedom of the Press and to maintain and improve its standards. To achieve this, the Council is empowered to help newspapers and news agencies to maintain their independence, to build up a code of conduct for them and to keep journalists in line with this code of conduct. It is a self-regulatory body whose decisions act as a guide and a code of ethics for journalists. It has played a magnificent role in indicting governments indulging in the suppression of freedom of the Press and journalists guilty of scurrilous writings. Many in the profession and outside feel that Press Council of India (PCI) is toothless and has failed to deliver the goods. Those subscribing to this view have been campaigning for giving it "more teeth". While opinion is divided on the issue, Justice R.S. Sarkaria, the then Chairman of the Council was dead set against any such move and I am in full agreement with him. Punitive powers with the Press Council, says Sarkaria, call be misused, as these have to be enforced by another government agency. Further the Council's decisions will become appealable in courts and will defeat the very purpose for which it was established. As of now, legal redress is not available to those who complain to the Press Council.

This is not to suggest that the Council does not suffer from any infirmity. The first fatal flaw lies in its system of nominating members on this statutory body. Selection of candidates is done by a complicated and complex system that discriminates against journalists working outside New

Delhi. It also involves an element of chance as drawing of lots is resorted to for selecting the persons nominated by various bodies representing diverse interests. This is not only unscientific but also gives an opportunity to unscrupulous elements to gang up and enter this august body. Yet another weakness of the PCI is that it deals with only the print media. It is high time that a media council is set up with a transparent and judicious system of nominating members on it. The proposed media council should have the right to deal with print as well as electronic media.

CONTEMPORARY MEDIA LANDSCAPE

1

MEDIA AND SOCIAL RESPONSIBILITY

RADHYE SHYAM SHARMA

We are passing through a period of "Information Explosion". This is the age of information. The electronic media, particularly satellite channels have completely changed the media scenario. All informations have now been reaching in the homes. This has not only changed the psychology of people but also changed their approach and life style in offices as well as in homes. With the revolution in communication technology, any information can reach in every part of the world within no time. The information explosion has particularly affected the minds of the young generation.

The information revolution has also changed the thinking process throughout the world. The whole approach and emphasis has taken altogether a new turn. During eighties and nineties, economic factors had displaced military power as the prime arbiter. The best examples of the results of this development are the ascendancy of Japan and Germany, in the world power structure. In fact once Germany's currency saved Dollar in the world market. The economic strength of then West Germany was responsible mainly for re-unification of both Germanys. The primacy of economic factor also played a major part in the dissolution of the Soviet Empire. The people inside the iron curtain came to know the realities of the world. The dictatorship of the proletariat could not resist its people from demanding more freedom and fulfilment of needs.

The population, land mass and natural resources are

now no more big power potential. These are the old concepts. In the modern world, technology quality has greater and bigger role than even Industrial Revolution. The information revolution and communication technology is now playing a bigger role.

On international level, the trend began to set to suit the industrially advanced countries and legitimised the conquest of empires. This in turn enabled these countries, many of which lacked natural resources to augment their shortfalls from their empire. The heavier dependence on technology, naturally led to economic attributes taking the second place gradually without challenging as yet the emerging primacy of military attributes. An example of this apparent waning of the importance of population and land mass in the power equation was transformation of Britain that lacked these basic attributes into Great Britain.

With the advent of Information Technology revolution the world is fashioning itself into a knowledge-based power structure.

One important fact is that Information Revolution has helped in globalisation. People today know more about the world today than few decades back. That is why there is also a talk of cultural invasion. However, it is difficult to remain aloof in present world and different cultures will have their impact on others. There are attempts to keep different communities and their cultural identities intact by emotional appeal or by fanaticism. Even then it is difficult to resist the impact of other cultures or thoughts because of information explosion. The Iron Curtain of Soviet Union could not resist the pressure of people to have freedom of expression and free economy. Information revolution in fact prepared ground for it.

When Mr. Rupert Murdoch arrived in Japan in June 1996, the Media Executives there, were puzzled. His visit was termed as unexpected invasion of foreign capital and its advance into their turf. Murdoch bought 21 per cent of prestigious Asahi T.V. The Japanese Prime Minister Ryutaro Hashimoto then commented that Mr. Murdoch's entry into Japan was natural in line with a global trend. Such trend is visible throughout the world today and it is bound to affect social, national and individual life styles as well as thinking process.

The Information Explosion has changed the look, content and presentation of newspapers. The TV has helped people in making their opinion after seeing events on the screen. This has affected their thinking process and approach towards life. TV has today become a powerful medium of communication. Thus, its role has become very important. The information explosion has brought more openness. This has also affected the political and social systems and the market. No government can now keep its people in the dark or in any illusion. People can see the happenings in any corner of the world with the help of electronic media and they can form their own opinion. Due to information explosion all types of controls on the flow of information have become almost impossible. The flow of information has also been responsible for changes in the society. This has also accelerated the pace of technological development and economic progress. The Information Technology Revolution has greater impact on Agricultural and Industrial Revolution. Both the revolutions have affected man's life and living. All the three have also been major civilization revolutions.

The main function of media, including TV, has been to inform and educate people. The films and TV added the new function of entertainment to it. But there is very thin line between entertainment and proper communication as the market forces have started dominating the media, particularly the TV. As there are large number of satellites and TV channels, they try to attract the advertisers. The manufacturers have found TV to be the most effective media to sell their goods by the help of advertisements and sponsored serials. To make their programmes attractive and popular they attach glamour to it. The overdose of sex and violence in programmes has become the order of the day. This all had its effect on the minds of the younger generation. With arrival of foreign media on large scale, it is said, that there is cultural invasion. This has changed the life style and also food habits of the people. Consumerism and commercialization have also changed their living habits. It is often alleged that we are drifting away from our own culture and identity. Western culture has been dominating the lifestyle. Thus, sometimes it is felt that people lose respect for their own culture.

The market forces know their target market. They have turned the whole media into a big business. Both newspapers and electronic media have become tools in the hands of market forces who are using them for earning more and more profits. The newspaper field is no more a mission. It has become a profession, rather an industry. Due to revolution in printing, communication and information technology, there is vast change in the newspapers. Now more emphasis is on sale and advertisements. The Institution of Editors is eroding and the management is dominating. The earnings through advertisements decide the policy of the newspapers. Advertisements do more than sell products or services. They also sell story of their times. The advertisements, and their styles show country's commercial history, its changing social mores rid life styles, its fads and fancies and trends. To increase the circulation, newspapers resort to sensationalism and sex in their advertisements. Many periodicals publish-naked or half-naked photos of women to attract more readership. Some TV channels sometimes resort to blue films, which include the publicity of their product. There is more of cheap entertainments than education. The standard of programmes is sometimes very low. They have to see that consumer buys only their product. They have to exist in competitive free market.

The advertisers also adopt same tactics. Sometimes the quantum of advertisements in a serial is so much that it becomes disgusting to see it. With the entry of multinationals and liberalism, the market forces have become stronger. They have been dominating in both the social as well as economic fields. This will give rise to economic exploitation. In our country where large population lives below poverty line, rise in consumerism and domination of market forces will increase disparities. The social tensions will also increase. In the race for profits through advertising, there is always a tendency to compromise with social values. The cut throat competition gives rise to underhand tactics. The market forces always bring pressures on producers to change the programmes to suit their needs. The episodes full of sex, crime and violence are repeated very often. This creates tensions in the society. The vulgarity spoils social atmosphere.

The communication is a means, which can be used both ways. Through this the society gets entertainment and information. The information can be concerning education, agricultural development, social upliftment, national integration, social and human values, national defence, liberation from poverty and backwardness and growth of an individual personality. The same media can be used for selfish interests only to earn money and worldly property at any cost. The market forces have no concern to see that people develop a scientific temper, which is very much needed today, as this is the age of science and technology. If the mind is not trained to use modern means in the interest of humanity then the evil mind can lead to disasters. This is what happening today. Inspite of material progress and information explosion there is no end to conflicts, wars, unrest, exploitation, colonial tendencies and profiteering and lack of justice.

It is the duty of the media to change this trend by using communication and information techniques in a way which can uplift human mind. It is to be seen that market forces are kept within control and do not go out of control. The economy is for the people and for the society. Society is not for economy. The market forces have to look into the interests of the society. Uncontrolled and cheap advertisements and selling substandard goods through wide publicity is a crime. The media has to decide as to which advertisements are worth carrying and which can damage the social fibre. The national and social interests have to be safeguarded. The history shows that the country became slave when foreign powers captured political power through business. The producer is free to earn profits but money is not everything. The needs of a healthy society and its future have to be kept in mind.

It was possible to run commercial traffic in TV. Commercial traffic meant more business and more rush for advertisements. It also meant millions more users every year and consequently an increase in demands for more goods. This was all due to Internet.

It is good that at some places the TV is being used for imparting education to students. The satellite system has also helped the scheme of distant education. Many channels are engaged in education programmes. This is encouraging. The market forces have to see that media also meets the requirement of the society. There has to be a balance between profit motive and welfare of the society. Market forces are a part of the whole system in the country. They cannot be kept above national interests. The media controlled by the government has also to be disciplined and properly used keeping in view the social values.

Media has to be responsible towards the country. It is also answerable to the society. No doubt it needs money to run itself. The advertisements are the biggest source of income. The market forces control the advertisement field and the government is also an important advertiser. It can create balance in this regard. The psyche of the market forces is to dominate the market and through it, dominate the economy. This cannot be allowed. The situation of free for all, can create economic and political anarchy. The media has to be used for constructive purposes also.

The need of the hour is to see that proper balance is kept between industrial production, consumption, market and sales. The economic development and human values, both have to be kept in mind. The media has a responsibility to create an atmosphere and thinking to keep that balance. Only media can do it. The TV channels and cable operators will have to resist the pressures of market forces. The government media can come to the aid of the saner elements who are running such channels.

2

COMMUNICATION TECHNOLOGY AND MEDIA EDUCATION

M.R. DUA

News, views, current affairs, business commerce, industry, travel, weather, instant messaging, chat, discussions, music, jobs, movies, personal finance, shopping, classifieds, astrology, entertainment, games—would you want more? Wait for some more time. The Net will provide it all, and much more!

Thanks to mind-boggling technology. Technology is the heart and soul of the present and future of all journalism and mass communication. In fact, it is hard to envision successful operation of any worthwhile area of mass communication without adequate and appropriate support of technology. The greatest gift of today's technology undoubtedly is the internet and its intimate ally, on-line journalism. Though the Net has brought the whole world on our home-screen, on-line journalism is instrumental in bringing in a jiffy up-to-date information from any nook and cranny of the globe any time of the day and night, just for the asking.

As we step into the twenty-first century, it is not only journalism and mass communication which witness technology rule, human life in its totality will almost completely hinge on it in every conceivable manner.

Talking of mass media, let us begin at the beginning. Print journalism, for example, has been completely transformed in all its gamut. Gone definitely are the days of hot metal. Remember Morse system of telegraphy for transmitting the news, manual typewriters and the dead phones! Hand composing, mono-type, lino-type are all now found in today's several mass media museums. Printing is computer-controlled, and all process of cutting, binding, packing, loading are computer-based everywhere.

Besides, gathering, processing and transmitting news from the point of origination to the user anywhere in the world are all handled strictly by sophisticated computers with the active assistance of faxes, cell phones, satellites criss-crossing the skies every minute of the day and night all over the globe. Technology controls and delivers effectively and efficiently, practically every stage and process of the working of today's any mass medium-radio, television-cable, satellite, internet, you name it.

What do all these developments bode for us—teachers and communicators? It should be amply understood by all of us, particularly teachers, that if education, training and research in journalism and mass communication have to be relevant and ably play their requisite roles in any nation-building activity, teachers will have to yoke and adopt technology in all its glory and agony in our academic and research programmes. The time is today and now. Any delay will be dangerous, if not fatal. Technology will not wait. As I say all this, technology is leapfrogging and encompassing every single activity of mass communication. We all know that computers which were some sort of novelty until the other day, are now found to be controlling, dictating and even laying down standard for human behaviour and our life style in every meaningfully imaginable way. It will not be far from truth to say that technology has redefined and prescribed not only the patterns we live by, but at the same time the way we think, act and have our being. As the time passes, new and new technologies keep emerging and converging providing extraordinary parameters and unheard dimensions to human issues and problems. The end result is the age that ICE (Information, Communication, Entertainment/ Education) is on us in its full pervasiveness. Instead of relying on a number of gadgets and media for ICE, technologists are trying to work out a single unit which delivers multiple functions. This gadget or device will be consumer-friendly, cost-effective and convenient. For example, a single unit cellular phone now provides far and near connections live, works as a fax, provides internet service and can also bring instant radio and television programming anywhere, anytime and as long as one wants. In addition, technology is now converging to provide value-added services, almost unheard of in India until recently. Telecommunication is rapidly intruding the arena of mass communication without any impunity. And, this overlapping is providing added facilities to the consumer. Be it broadcasting or print, for instance, you don't have to store these for future use. Just go to the relevant website and you will get the items of your interest right in front of you on the screen. Read them, print them and/or just restore them.

While in India's most journalism schools and mass communication departments, computers and internets are not yet in popular use as abroad. We will have to prepare most of our students for rapid advancement in such technologies. It is worth stating here that in 1999-2000, India's ICE industry and all associated technologies with a revenue of over Rs. 18,000 crore paved the way for internet : from 0.27 million connections in 1998-1999, the total number increased to 8.0 million connections in 1999-2000, and is expected to multiply to 23 million connections by the year 2003. Moreover, the internet has introduced an e-generation of ISPs (Internet Service Providers), dot.coms, e-commerce and software solution providers. Again, as of June 2000, approximately 62 new ISPs have already started operations. In addition, 243 new licences are believed to have been issued. Thus, the future awaits mind-boggling expansion in ICE where our students, and we as ordinary communicators, will have to find our feet. Moreover, technology leapfrogs at a tremendous speed and volume. If we do not keep pace with new innovations and emerging techniques, our loss will be irreparable. We must take a serious note of the fact that ICE revolution in India in the future will be led by Interactive and value-added service that would revolutionise the way we utilize the Net.

While internet and computers keep churning out amazingly, newer and newer techniques and unfolding unknown horizons, television companies, cable and satellite continue launching new channels and exploring obscure avenues. For example, India's premier channel, Subhash Goel's Zee Telefilms, is offering zeenext.com, which is an aggregation of e-services, zeelearn.com, a part of its education convergence strategy, according to a recent report in the press.

One could go on and on. But the fact of the matter is that communication technology is sooner than later bound to usher in a devastating whole new environment. All this is certain to impact profusely the way future journalism and mass communication media of our country are to shape. It is time we perceive these dimensions and parameters, lest we are taken unaware.

However, it would be extremely essential and indeed prudent to take note of the negative aspects of technology of media, as it appears before us today. As the present and emerging technologies unlock newer and newer benedictions and secrets of humanity, we have to be conscious of the fact that it is technology and an abundance of its that creates fresh demands for excellence on media-persons. There are serious questions of cut throat competition within and without the print, audio and visual media of mass communication. These have to be met competently and squarely, failing which the society will flounder for survival. These are controversial and burning issues of sex, violence and horror shows. Then, there is quality or lack of parental guidance, societal pressures and state controls, which sometimes measure to non-sensical limits. Then, there are national boundaries and international vested interests which render sky limits redundant and irrelevant. For, technology has its own unorthodox proportions and dimensions.

Pornography and unashamedly naked shows shock the oriental audiences. But, there are no ways to jam these. Advertising of harmful products such as liquor and tobacco make their own killing on the media. While technology brings all these in our bedrooms and drawingrooms, mechanism has yet to be innovated to prevent these, if required. Moreover, the issues of privacy of information, of security, consumer rights, and most important, one's creditworthiness through the Net. These are some of the serious and very grey areas.

Besides, cinema which was earlier a kind of fodder for television is moving away and trying to recoupe and retrieve its fan following. Though there are revivals in cinema industry's fortunes, but empty halls and the flops galore. Nonetheless, the cinema in India is certainly inching towards new pastures and conquering new heights. This surely is because technology has mesmerised the cinegoer no end. For he wants to watch the shows with innumerable awe-inspiring effects, trick, and mixed vision on the big screen. Thus, we see that all round the technological revolution has and will further transform mass media operations and education, training and research radically. Are we, educators and practitioner ready to meet the challenge? Time is now to be ready and prepare ourselves so that the next generation of the students rise to the occasion and are able to get astride.

3

MEDIA IN CONFLICT SITUATION

JAISHRI N. JETHWANEY

When we talk of media in a conflict situation, we generally think that media "behave" differently in abnormal or conflict situations. We tend to prejudge the role or rather, the negative role played by the media in a crisis situation. This inference is based on the general belief that – "Good news is no news" for the media and the media thrive on the sensational, the scandalous and juicy copy. Before we talk about the role of media, let us discuss the conflict or the crisis *per se*

A conflict or a crisis is described as an abnormal situation, an untoward happening which needs resolution. In other words—Management.

A crisis situation is like a many act play with a number of 'players' playing their designated role. Some players are primary while others are peripheral. The players comprise the people or institutions which are affected, the people or institutions which are supposedly responsible for the crisis, the people or institutions who set the agenda or are capable of influencing public opinion and the onlookers or the public at large.

Media's role, of late, in conflict situations especially in times of insurgency or terrorism has come into sharp focus. Before going into specifics, let us define terrorism, first. The Chambers dictionary defines terror as extreme fear, a terrorist as one who makes himself a nuisance and terrorism as an organized system of intimidation, especially for political ends. Terrorism comes in varying forms. There are state terrorism acts waged against the citizens or individuals who may not be recognized as citizens of that state such as the *Mohajirs* in Pakistan, state sponsored terrorism, against people of other states; and insurgent terrorism. In this kind of terrorism the "Violence is mainly perpetrated for its effects on others (rather) than the immediate victims" (Schmid & De Graaf, 1982.)

Paletz and Viscon feel, the insurgent terrorism, may not be as deadly as state terrorism, nor its victims as numerous. It has, however, achieved far more visibility and provoked an extensive often passionate and polemical, literature. (Paletz L. David and Viscon C. Danielle; *Terrorism and the Media,* 1992).

The use of the word terrorism does not have universal application. In fact there is no consensus on what comprise terrorist activities. In the Indian context, some insurgent groups insisted not to be referred as such. We have seen the reactions of some of the militant groups in Punjab who insisted on being called the '*Kharkus*' and in Kashmir who term their acts of violence as *Jehad*. From their point of view, they have a definite role to play and probably acts of intimidation and terrorism against the people are considered by them as a means and a part of a strategy and not end unto itself. Whatever the reasons, but increasingly the usage of the word "terrorism" has dropped in favour of expressions such as "militancy" and "insurgency" by the media.

In the book *Political Terrorism*, Schmid, Jongman, *et al.* (1988) refer to a fundamental triangular relationship seen in terrorist strategy. This includes the terrorist, the target of the terrorist violence (such as the kidnapped people, the hostages in a plane, a killed by-passer), and the actual targets of the action, whose minds terrorists try to affect with their violence. This may include government of a country for seeking attention of the public in general or a section, which is put in a state of fear.

The acts of militants by and large aim at:

1. Demonstrating the worthlessness of the government;
2. Attracting public approval;
3. Creating chasms among different sections of society—

the ones' who support their actions, the others who do not, and also the fence-sitters who could be cajoled/attracted; and

4. Presenting their violent acts as acts of heroism.

Some scholars refer to insurgents' psychological goals. Carlos Marighella (1972), speaks of the "War of Nerves" as an aggressive strategy, in which "information, spread by the mass media and orally, is meant to demoralize the government".

Insurgents commit violent acts as hijacking of planes, killing of hostages, blowing up of rail tracks to achieve psychological results. They may have nothing against the actual victims of their violence *per se*.

The terrorist groups have realized that by using minimum resources they can achieve greater impact through media coverage. Some scholars have thus spoken of the complicity of media in the drama of terrorism. The media are 'stage-managed' by subversive groups, probably without their ever realizing it.

Here comes the role of the media. Hundreds of studies are conducted every year all over the world to gauge the role and impact of mass media which many believe have become all pervasive, omnipotent and all powerful. The history of research studies over the last half a century can, however be seen as an oscillation between the perspectives delineating the power of the media over its audience, and the perspectives which speak of the challenge of protecting the audience from the potential effects of the message.

Throughout the nineteenth century, when Penny Press hit the streets, the potential power of the mass press to persuade and manipulate the public and perhaps undermine the democratic process was felt and dreaded upon. By seeking the sensational, concentrating on personalities rather than news, the press, it was construed, was deliberately diverting the attention of the public, arousing irrational passions and lowering the esteem of certain institutions. However, it was not until World War I, and during the phase of the rise of Fascism and Nazism that the role of government in managing news and using propaganda as a vehicle of social control came to focus.

The advent of television in the 1960's and a virtual "invasion" from the skies in the 90s has made a great difference in the way we think and comprehend issues. Anne Rawley Saldich in her book "Electronic Democracy" is critical, almost fearful about the growing dependence of the masses on the electronic media, especially television in gathering information and their belief in what they see. She refers to television as a 'corridor of power'.

Are media objective? A lot of heated discussions have been held by scholars, researchers a concerned sections of the society from time to time. Walter Lippmann, the legendary news man felt that media do not reflect all the reality, they only spotlight parts of reality, depending on the perception of the reporters as to what constitutes news or what will be more impactful on the audience. The "agenda setting" role of the media has also come into sharp focus. Whether information received through the mass media changes attitudes or merely reinforces pre-existing beliefs might be less important than the role of the media play in determining what people will think about.

If we look at the media coverage of the insurgent acts in the 80's and the 90's in the Indian context, we find a very interesting behavioural pattern amongst the media institutions. No full fledged research studies covering the above issues in the 80's when insurgency and intimidation was at its peak in some States and the simmering trouble in Kashmir in the 90's seem to have been conducted. However, as an avid consumer of the media, one can surely say that the mainstream media especially, the print has certainly applied self imposed codes on themselves about covering insurgency. From an emotional to by and large responsible reporting could be seen over a period of time. One of the reasons could be that the coverage gave undue publicity to the perpetrators of violence. They also probably realized that people suffer from "Information Immunity' when they hear, read or watch same or similar things over a period of time.

During the infamous emergency in India in the seventies, news was censored. A few newspapers refused to print the censored news. Instead, their editorials went blank. The *Statesman* and the *Indian Express* are a few cases in point. At the height of insurgency in Punjab, some of the militant groups intimidated the media to print their points of view.

Some newspapers bowed down, others did not. Those who did not, risked their lives. The editor of *Punjab Kesari*, the Station Director of All India Radio, Chandigarh, and Station Director of Doordarshan at Srinagar among many others faced the bullets.

At times, intellectuals, social scientists and concerned citizenry, have pointed out the question of complicity i.e. whether the media are participants and not mere observers, as referred above. On the issue of reservations for the OBCs, in 1990, when youngsters torched themselves by dozens in different parts of the country, many felt that it was the glamour and glitz of the initial event (an aflame Rajiv Goswami's pictures splashed in the media all over) that attracted the youngsters to self-immolation than the real cause.

It is a fact that various insurgent groups have used media more often to their advantage, if we were to compare it with other groups engaged in the task of nation-building. But then the insurgents also feel that they are equally responsible people. It is the state, which does not understand them!

During the Kargil Crisis in 1999, one of the studies on media content analysis reflected that the Indian media by and large were swayed by the national fervour. Objective reporting in a way suffered at the cost of emotion. Celebrated editor, Prabhash Joshi said in a conference that "absolute objectivity is an absolute farce".(Jethwaney & Sarkar Communicator Vol. XXXIV No. 3, July-Sept, 1999 (An Indian Institute of Mass Communication publication).

Can there be a code of conduct on the part of the media in situations such as these? Can media be regulated or should it be regulated by the State? Or should the codes be self-imposed, are some of the issues that need addressing.

Paletz and Tawney suggest five levels, ranging from an absence of guidelines to detailed codes:

Level 1 No rules for covering terrorism; no guidelines, codes, or even approaches.

Level 2 No rules, but philosophies or general policies about how to cover terrorism.

Level 3 No rules for terrorism. But general programming rules for coverage of violence and civil disorders.

Level 4 Standardized guidelines.

Level 5 Detailed rules, codes, guidelines.

(Paletz L. David and Tawney & Laura, *Terrorism and the Media*, 1992)

Schmid refers to the three realms of reality from the editor's perspective viz,

1. The real objective world (whatever is happening "out there").
2. The symbolic world (mainly the world portrayed and presented in the media).
3. The subjective world (the world as people interpret it in their minds). (*Ibid.*, p. 111).

Mercifully, the media in India especially the print are as free as media in any other democratic country and thanks to the proliferation of the satellite channels, the news bulletins on Doordarshan are also getting professional. Hence more credible.

As the societies are getting more and more complex and chasms among various stakeholders increasing, the media would often find themselves more embroiled. There are already question marks on the objectivity of media reporting especially in critical times. Some media houses in the West have prepared a code of conduct for covering insurgency.

The Indian media can consider some of the following:

1. To report objectively, keeping in view different perspectives of various "players".
2. To report comprehensively and not merely "spotlight", so that the audience have a fair idea about the conflicting viewpoints.
3. To maintain editorial independence. While most of the media organizations have a definite line of thinking, in matters such as insurgency, it is better to have a neutral approach for all. The "player's" truth must prevail.
4. To humanize reporting. Statistics alone can have brutal impact on the psyche of the audience. In insurgent situations also, there are always 'oasis in desert'. The media need to look for them and report human-interest stories.
5. Not to serve as spokesperson for an insurgent or insurgent group.
6. Never volunteer to solve a problem. That is for the governments and not the media.
7. To be first with the news. In this age of information when information is not the prerogative of the chosen few, only those will survive who are fast, transparent and consistent with editorial and reportage ethics.

With a complex social structure, the emergence of the new world order, the information age over-load that most of us are suffering from, it is only pertinent that media define a definite role for themselves—as watchdogs, agenda setters, information disseminators or moulders of public opinion. Whether these can be taken in isolation or in combination is a debatable point. Coverage of conflict situations, however, will continue to be the Litmus Test for the media.

4

DOT COM JOURNALISM

B.K. KUTHIALA

In 1994 Leo S. Bogart describing the media system in a perfect world of tomorrow stated that the mass media system should have the following qualities:

Freedom : Every impulse, experience and belief of every human being should be available for expression and examination without any restriction, regulation or censorship.

Range and Variety : The content of the media should have the maximum possible diversity of the coverage of topics and every topic must be treated in a manner which allows the plurality of thoughts and views.

Balance : The purpose of the media would be to create a wide data base for the receivers and the task of making opinions, views and attitudes is to be left to the people. There should also be a balance between entertainment and information with a provision of multiplicity of sources.

Innovativeness : The media system should permit a regular flow of new ideas, styles, formats and give them a chance to be patternised by the audience.

Competitiveness : Any kind of monopoly in media systems should be resisted both in delivery and content. The system should be structured to encourage entrepreneurship.

Accessibility : The mass media should be so structured and technologies adapted in such a manner so that mass media is available equally to all. Bogart added that this may require expanding the existing media systems.

Quality : The media system should strive to attain

standards of excellence in conception and execution. But any attempt which fall short of the given quality may not be suppressed.

Bogart further warns that the last feature of quality is most controversial because setting standards of excellence in the field of mass communication can be risky. An important idea may be poorly presented while a flimsy idea slickly packaged in a TV sound bite, for example, might be misleading. Therefore, in a free society there is no scope for any authority to pass judgement on what ideas can be offered to the people. But in a perfect media system, according to Bogart the goal would not be to suppress the bad but to encourage the good.

Digitalisation of Data

The last decade of the 20th century has provided to the mankind the technical options that could virtually assure creation of any kind of mass media systems. Digitalisation of data, delivered by dramatic new switching techniques and fibre optics to home and work place offers access to infinite amount of material within a matter of seconds. The internet systems are virtually entire libraries at home, at our fingertips. The new technologies have altered the basic nature of mass communication which is almost one way flow of information to an interactive media system. In fact computers, internet, satellites etc. are the technologies of freedom.

It is generally believed that the greatest revolution has taken place in the mode of transmission. Once communication messages: news, news analysis, articles, editorials, programmes of music, visuals, spoken words, graphics and animation etc. are digitalised i.e. reduced to computer coded zeroes and ones, then they can be transmitted through a variety of channels. This means a very vast change. But the change may not take place in the media of mass communication so much as in the digitalisation of the content. Nicholas Negroponte, Director of Media Lab at the Massachusetts Institute to Technology, explains :

> In the old days, we considered newspapers and television very different media; this is changing rapidly. Newspapers begin as digitalised information collected by reporters, edited by editors and eventually transformed into ink squeezed auto paper. By the turn of the century, all television will also be digital.

With digital technology it is possible to personalise the mass media. The television screen will show what we want to see. The radio will tell the news which is important for the listeners only. If you want to watch a television serial the system will recommend an excellent one just as your friend would have.

Digitalisation will affect individual media in different ways but in ways unique to each media. Moreover, each operation of the media will have its own technology and altered practices. In this chapter we will confine to some of the changes that have taken place or are likely to occur in the field of journalism.

1. New Collection

In traditional schools of Journalism till about few years ago the students were given special training in shorthand and typewriting. But gradually the reporters and correspondents started using mini-taperecorders and the need to note down the news on the spot on a paper vanished. The practice continues with more sensitive and sophisticated audio recorders. In print media use of light sensitive films is being replaced by digital cameras which do not need specialised training.

The process of news collection at the level of reporters and correspondents is also changing. News persons can send information on e-mail. The practice of distributing press releases is also gradually being replaced first by the use of fax and then by e-mail. Moreover, whatever the organisation wishes to share with media is available on the websites as and when required. The dynamic websites are considered to be more media friendly.

The reporter is better equipped today to provide background on the news topics. Whatever has been reported by him earlier is available on the computer and if more information is required it is available on internet. Still further efficient telephony coupled with internet provides for instantaneous interaction with the sources. Perhaps more important is the mode of filing a news report. No more telegrams, couriers and teleprinters. The story is filed on a PC and get distributed to the bureau and news-room immediately. Even the photographs are being digitalised and transmitted. The result is obvious, the newspapers are now more visual.

The important thing to note here is that the time for collecting the information and filing a story has been reduced drastically so that the field reporters have more time to file more stories thereby increasing the diversity in the content of the newspapers. The nightmares of the old generation journalists of faulty telephones and telegrams is a thing of the past.

The communication between the newsroom and field reporters is also increased both qualitatively and quantitatively. There were times when an editor or a member of the editorial team would have direct contact with the field reporters very rarely but today it is almost a daily practice and in many cases more than once a day. The result of all these innovative practices is reflected in the newspapers where, of late, more topics are covered and each topic is covered in greater detail.

2. On the Desk

The traditional practice of receiving the teleprinter copy or typed or handwritten news stories is in the news-room of the paper is almost non existent today. The magician in the process of news production, the sub-editor, today hardly uses a paper or a pen or pencil. In an ideal news-room system the news received by the news editor on the monitor is distributed for subbing on the computers connected in the form of intranet (LAN) to various sub-editors. The symbols of subbing—delete, caps, insert, right-left align etc. are now lost. The sub-editing is done on the computer screen using various tools and routines provided with the world processing softwares. The most important change that has taken place in the news-room is that the copy is not subbed and given to compositor or data entry operator. The real subbing is carried out by sub-editor himself or herself. The sub-editor has also access to the previous stories on the related subjects and can pad the stories more efficiently. Moreover, the actual column space that would be occupied in the story can also be seen on the screen. The sub-editor no more writes instructions for the headlines about the type and the size of the font to be used but writes the headlines according to the width of the story and reduces or increases the size of the type according to the space available. Range of type faces available has also widened.

One of the most important qualities of the news persons working on the desk was their language proficiency and expertise in spellings. Today a simple operation of spell check performs the task. Even the syntax and the grammar of sentence specially in English can be checked on the computer itself automatically.

The pictures, graphics and maps can be directly received from the source or scanned and adjusted according to the space available using the basic principles of design.

3. Page Make-up

In many newspapers today the practice of physical cutting and pasting for preparing the page becomes absolute known. Two of systems have evolved over the years. Firstly, each page of the newspaper is allotted to a specific person on the desk who receives the stories, performs the task of the sub-editing and then prepares the page on the screen itself. The page is directly sent to the printing department. The other practice is that the news stories are allotted according to the specialisation of the sub-editors and finally persons specifically engaged for the page make-up prepares the pages on the screen and sends them to the printing department. Although some national newspapers are still engaged in the practice of cutting and pasting, with the introduction of the new technology of computer to plate more operations are likely to be deleted and the time gap between the finalisation of the page and the actual print out of the newspaper has reduced considerably.

The entire process of subbing on the screen and preparing the pages on the screen itself is not only a task in which no paper is used but it is also a time saving practice. Rough estimates will indicate that the task which earlier took an hour now takes only 47 minutes with the introduction of computer. With increased proficiency and better managed systems is that the time to 'go to bed' of the newspaper has now gone almost upto midnight. This ensures the coverage of the stories that occurred even late night. In some cases it has been noted that an event that happened even around 11.00 p.m. was found published in the newspaper which reached the reader at 5.00 a.m.

Another consequence of automation of news-room of worth mentioning here is preparation of pages at different centres. The reporters and correspondents today not only file the stories but they may be expected to send the stories in the form in which they want them published i.e. arranged in columns with headlines. In important centres the pages may be prepared and electronically sent to the central point for publication. Even further the entire pages may be published at the centre of the collection of the news and then attached with the main newspaper in the morning. *Dainik Bhaskar* in this part of the country has innovated in this respect and prepares pages pertaining to the centres covering local news, publishes there and then only. This has resulted in a very wide coverage of local news so much so that in some cases domestic quarrel between husband and wife also finds place in the local news because everyday certain amount of space needs to be filled. Theoretically we can say that the news values are also changing.

4. Publishing and Distribution

With the introduction of computers in the news-room the printing section gets the pages of the newspaper all ready for printing on the computer itself. In establishments where the negatives and positives are to be prepared for plate making the camera ready copy is taken. But in situations where computer to plate technology has been introduced the plate is prepared electronically and then put on the printing machine.

Today the newspapers are more colourful because of the advancement in the technology of printing. But the computer helps to decide the colour schemes and also helps to reproduce the photographs in original colours. Supplements published by some of the newspapers are real creations of art of design. They exhibit full use of types and white space with colours and graphics. A person with an artistic eye not only enjoys the content of the supplements but appreciates the artistic creativity also.

An innovation that is being talked about these days in the field of publishing is print-on-demand. This is customised publishing and means that the entire newspaper, magazine or book is available on an electronic device and required number of copies can be produced as and when needed. One can also visualise the future where a reader specifies his requirements of the content also and a newspaper catering to the specific needs be delivered. For example, a person can express his desire to receive news about sports, share market and cultural activities and everything that happened during last 24 hours in these fields will be delivered to him in the form of a newspaper.

5. Internet Newspaper

Today almost all newspapers of significance have an internet edition. The time at which internet edition is available on the computers is slightly earlier than the time when the printed newspapers are distributed and there is a competition between newspapers to advance the time of the publication of internet edition of the newspapers. This has helped the non-resident Indians and visitors abroad to browse the Indian newspapers even when they are thousands of miles away. But the scope of internet journalism is likely to have its independent existence. There are going to be newspapers available only on internet and the dream of a newspaper without a paper will become a reality. The striking feature of such newspapers will be that it will be a time-less newspaper in the sense that the news stories and other content will be added to these newspapers as and when ready. The newspaper will not be bound in the number of pages and it will be constantly updated so that the information will be disseminated instantaneously. Furthermore, we will have newspapers with live coverage of the events. Still further, the newspapers will lend themselves not only to reading but a person can even listen to a newspaper and can also watch whatever is reported in animated or real mode.

Another direction in which journalism is likely to excel is in the field of media person and consumer interactivity. The readers are not satisfied only with the information that a media person decides to give to them. They may have quest for more information, or clarification to seek. The electronic journalism provides for two-way communication and interactive journalism is not a far cry. It is already happening when *India Today* makes available its media persons for a chat on internet on fixed days and timings. This is likely to expand and a dialogue between the media persons and the readers is going to increase. This may be taken an extension of the columns devoted to letters to editor.

Another very interesting scenario can also be visualised. The actors in the news stories may be accessible to the consumers of the news and media persons may act as facilitators to create a dialogue between the persons who actually make news and the person who consume the information. In such a scenario the role of media person is entirely changed. The new role is that of a coordinator or a facilitator.

6. Training Needs

Only some of the developments in journalism that are taking place or likely to occur in the near future have been outlined above. Much more is possible and perhaps sky is the limit. But an important task that needs the attention of the trainers and teachers of journalism and mass communication is to comprehend and analyse these changes and then prepare the training and teaching systems to cater to the new requirements.

As of today it is very unfortunate that though the newspaper industry is totally computerised some of the journalism departments do not have a component of computer training in their syllabi. Recently there was a requirement for 'online sub-editors' in a magazine, they failed to find them, because the departments of Journalism and Mass Communication in the Universities have not trained their students for such tasks. Though the journalistic practices have changed drastically the course contents of the journalism courses remains static. Therefore, there is a need to reorient the teaching and training for the present requirements. It would be a suicidal if we fail to visualise the future and prepare for it.

A new area of a very attractive employment that has emerged during last few months is of content development. So many websites are being created and the software engineers only know how to prepare them but what information is to be given and how it is to be presented is nobody's and everybody's job. The students of the departments of Mass Communication are best suited to perform such jobs as they are proficient in language and in arranging the information in a manner which enables the consumers to go for maximum eyeballs. But this task requires exposure to the technology of website designing. If we add the subject of website designing and content development in our courses not only the students will get more and better employment we shall be contributing our bit in this revolution of electronics. Same is the case with internet advertising. Many such cases for the need for a new look on the teaching and training of mass communication can be given. But for preparing for such a change in the curricula the teachers also need to be exposed to these technologies. Unfortunately this is not happening.

We have also to keep in mind the emerging trends in the field of mass communication during last decade. Today a professional mass communicator moves from one medium to another with ease. The professional is less concerned about the specific branch—print medium-radio-television, advertising, public relations or internet. The main task is to prepare strong messages that can be presented to audiences by whatever means available.

Ronald T. Farrar has recommended that the students planning to work in mass communication can expect to change carried—*not jobs, carriers*—many times. Therefore, the students need to be trained to be flexible and adaptable to new circumstances. Farrar suggests that a student should possess, at a minimum, the following :

1. Clear and effective writing skills.
2. A familiarity with more than one medium of mass communication.
3. A strong set of ethical and professional values.

5

ONLINE JOURNALISM
Strengths and Weaknesses

SHEETAL THAPAR

No other age would well qualify to be an age of technology than the present one. Change has become the order of life so much so that old institutions are decaying and new institutions are being born in as short a period as a decade. People who have been documenting these changes have been so much overwhelmed by the rapidity of these changes that they themselves have felt outmoded enough to attempt such an undertaking.[1] In the history of thoughts or theory building, concepts have changed so often that what was regarded modern at one stage is considered stale now. The concept of modernity itself has become an unjustifiable enterprise and post-modernism looms over the horizon of public life in an imposing and ineffaceable form.

In the sphere of journalism too, which contributes and supports the shaping of an age through its information gathering and disseminating functions, technology has made heavy inroads. While information gathering is no longer the exclusive preserve of human beings, information dissemination has been almost overtaken by the marriage of communication and information technology. In fact, what we see and how we see is being shaped more often by technology than by human effort and if we were to stretch the point, we would agree with McLuhan that technology has become the 'other half' of (wo)man in so far as it is an extension of the various sensory and motor organs of the self.

Historical Background

The emergence of online journalism has not been an abrupt event. It has been evolving through three stages. Initially, newspaper establishments looked at the internet only as a means to have an electronic presence, and in many cases it was a me-too kind of situation. Those who were looking for just a presence on the net did not invest much and that got reflected in their sites; online journalists mostly reformatted content from their mother ship. In stage two, which gained momentum last year and characterizes most of the better news sites, the journalists create original content and augment it with such additives as hyperlinks (with which a reader can instantly access another website); interactive features such as search engines, which seek out material on specific topics; and a degree of customization—the ability to choose what categories of news and information you receive. The credit for this goes to television channels like CNN and NBC which changed the rules of the game. With a different velocity of news, sites like CNN interactive and MSNBC provide instant news, taking advantage of the news gathering machine they have for their 24-hour news channels. These channels are giving a tough time to the newspapers on the internet which update their sites once in a day, following their print cycles.

Stage three is just beginning to emerge at only a handful of sites. It is characterized by original news content designed specifically for the web as a new medium of communication. Stage three will be characterized by a willingness to rethink the nature of a 'community' online and, most important, a willingness to experiment with new forms of storytelling. Often this is 'immersive' storytelling, which allows you to enter and navigate through news report in ways different from just reading it. Sometimes this might be done through new technology. An example: Rob Fixmer, editor of *Cyber Times*, says that *The New York Times* is experimenting with omni-directional imaging, which would permit you to explore a 360-degree field of vision. Such technology will allow viewers the experience of 'entering' a live or recorded news event, or to see a still or moving photo in three dimensions, thus, providing the advantage of being a participant observer.[2]

In the context of the changing face of journalism, this study, *Online Journalism : Strengths and Weaknesses,* attempts to analyze the strengths and weaknesses of online journalism in terms of the process/institution itself and the beneficiaries/end users of online journalism.

The discussion has been divided into two sections—first dealing with the process/institutional aspect of the impact of online journalism and the second dealing with the impact of online journalism on the beneficiaries/end users.

I

As already mentioned, online journalism is a Frankenstein born out of the wedlock of modern technology and journalism, so any discussion of the impact of online journalism on the process or institution itself must take a look at the technology underpinning it and the freedom of information that it espouses.

The technology that online journalism rides on is unlike that which preceded it. The earlier communication technologies helped in the dispersion of information from a central hub of the news-room to a wide mesh of news consuming audience through mass publication or broadcasting of news. The technology of online journalism makes a marked departure from the mass targeting technology to an individualized technology that has the potential of reaching out to a greater audience without being insensitive to the idiosyncrasies of the individual news consumers. Thus, this technology negotiates a change from 'massification' to 'individuation' of news.

This in itself is an imposing prospect that can be both beneficial and deleterious. By opening the flood gates of interpretations and re-interpretations of news through a unique joint effort of the news makers and the news consumers in the process of news making, what has also been referred to as the diaspora of meaning in the post-modernist terminology, it holds out the prospect of an infinity of meanings. This multiplicity of meanings can be beneficial in that it would aid the construction of new reality based on otherwise swept-under-the-carpet truths. But it can also be dangerous as it might lead to chaos of meanings and conflicts of miscommunication.

So far as its impact on freedom of information is concerned, online journalism seems to be a blessing in disguise. It seeks to realize the avowed aim of journalism, namely upholding the citizen's right to freedom of information, in a much more effective way than the traditional form of journalism. The hosting of news-based websites is not as investment heavy an enterprise as the establishment of a news channel or newspaper. This has a liberating effect on 'intellectual property' which till now was yoked to physical property, what is often called 'capital' in business terminology. The liberation of intellectual property implies the assertion of the news professionals who can on their own without much capital host their own news-based websites. The coming into their own of the news professionals holds out the promise of greater professional commitment and freedom from the constraining effects of what is called market-driven journalism. Besides, the mushrooming of news sites can provide multiple angles on current news which otherwise tend to get stifled through the gatekeeping function of the editorial section.

II

'The new papyrus' age has arrived with the paper virtually disappearing from the news-room. The revolution in technology brought about by internet in print media is changing even faster than the introduction of the computer. Cybernews comes in a sophisticated bundle of news, services and e-commerce. This is fundamentally a new paradigm and it changes the relationship between the journalist and the news consumer.

Updated Information

Online journalism promises more and updated news content than its traditional counterparts, most of it free. So it is not surprising that an increasing number of the world's forty to fifty million internet users are going online for their news.[3] For instance, over 1.1 million users accessed the MSNBC.com news website on August 17, 1998, the top story being Clinton-Lewinsky affair, when the President testified and addressed the nation on his relationship with Lewinsky. The record was broken when more than two million people accessed the site on September 12, 1998, when the *Star Report* was made public. On the same day, CNN Interactive reported three lakh hits a minute even before the report was on the net. And the decision of the Congress authorities to make available the entire report on the internet, turned out to be the net's biggest challenge as a medium to distribute data. Several million people downloaded the report and it was splashed on the front pages of Sunday newspapers all over the world, including those in India. This was the first major occasion when newspapers turned to the internet for data in a big way.[4] The other events that were instant hits on the internet in the recent past are riots and unrest in Indonesia, nuclear tests by India and Pakistan, and US bombings in Sudan and Afghanistan.

Some of the websites are going beyond their print counterparts. Newspapers follow a 24-hour cycle, so do their internet editions. But since internet is such a live medium, news sites are experimenting to keep pace with news in some ways. The *Deccan Herald* site runs a ticker line at the bottom of the screen that flashes the latest news, which the main paper will give in the next day's edition. This is normally breaking news, it is more like a news agency flash. Similarly, the *India Today Online* has developed a unique product that overcomes its inability to provide daily news since it is not a daily newspaper. The site has an independent product called *News Today*, a page that offers online news, updated four times a day. Some sites offer

BSE index opening and closings, and other online information from the markets.[5]

Hyperlinks

Online journalism features the utility of hyperlinks which is useful in both compressing and extending information depending on the reader's choice. The electronic cousin of a footnote belongs to a way of presenting information called hypertext. These are highlighted words or phrases, which when clicked, provide more information related to the given word or phrase. Then a window filled with new text pops up on the screen. But the extra material does not appear unless the reader asks for it.

However, one of the problems that handicaps current hypertext systems is that readers get lost. They make so many jumps away from the article they started reading that they cannot find their way back. This shows how alluring the jumping can be. But, as the readers get frustrated when they feel lost (they miss the control they are used to having with conventional print media), they are likely to desert the medium.[6] This is not a serious shortcoming as the reader can be kept oriented by use of the bookmark and the map. The reader can place an electronic bookmark anywhere in the current article and can come back in a few minutes or next week. The map is usually rendered as a linear list rather than a treelike diagram with many branching paths; it shows the readers where they have been.

Archival Facility

In an electronic world, the news hole is nearly infinite. There are no newsprint expenses, no dead trees. And nothing need ever disappear. The whole system is a giant morgue.

The online publications are a sort of value-added product. Some websites provide complete version of print publications along with archives that run back a year. *Indian Express Online* is one of them. *The Times of India* made available all the information contained in *Education Times*, along with the databases of Indian educational institutions on its site. *India Today's* comprehensive site on Indian elections was yet another example of value addition. The site presented reference material from past elections, results from the last four elections provided constituency-wise and party-wise, news provided state-wise and party-wise, portraits of candidates and several interesting contests. The *India Today Online* made available the Jain Commission's interim report on its site.[7] Similarly, some online papers cover cricket games live and budget as well.

Interactive Editions

On the net, a newspaper is no more just one-way traffic. They have become 'interactive'. In fact, more and more publications choose to call their internet editions as 'interactive editions' rather than internet editions. In an interactive newspaper you can see what you want, how much you want, the font size that you are comfortable with, you can see the details of advertisements which you wish and just zero-in to a particular item without going through all the pages. Refer a back issue with just a click of the mouse, participate in an opinion poll, express your opinion and send a feedback to the editor while you are reading the paper. This is the essence of interactive media.[8]

Internet news is, therefore, a dialogue with an identifiable audience, a global conversation on topics that can be broad, such as on a general news site, or laser-like specific, such as news, advice and products for animal trainers who use clickers. The news sites deliver more news and information—a bottomless source of help. They prompt you, provoke you, respond to you, by e-mail or e-mail newsletters.

There are online newspapers which have services like 'news by e-mail', where you just have to indicate the subject of your choice and they will keep sending you news and articles on that subject by e-mail.

Hits and Page Views

The popularity chart of a website is just a click away for the management. Number of hits recorded per day display the readership status and, thus, offers a scope for change in the light of this response.

The Indian Express gets 2.5 million hits a day. They also get 300 e-mails a day, some of which are published in the Letters to the Editor column. Similarly, the *India Today Online* gets two million 'page views' a month. The daily e-mail inflow is about 125 and half the letters published in the print edition are received via e-mail. *The Hindustan Times.com* gets over 100 e-mails a day. Visitors to *The Times of India* site are required to register, and fill in some personal details. This has helped the paper to build up a database on the profile of its readers, which in turn is shared with advertisers.[9] Similarly, CNN Interactive, the world's busiest news website records some 3.5 million page views a day.[10]

Emergence of Webzines

A new category of news providers, apart from newspapers and television channels, has also emerged on the internet. They are the webzines or netzines, which do not have a print or TV counterpart, but run news service on the internet.[11] The most formidable challenge to the traditional media (now turning to the net) is coming from the real online media (which has no print counterpart). The new challengers are technology companies and non traditional news/publishing companies. In terms of the competition that such new news genres provide to the existing media, it is a welcome development. But in so far as they are not professionally up to the mark, they hold out the bleak prospect of dilution of professional standards.

Shift from Anglo-American Centrism

While the internet has come largely from the US, it is generally the consensus that as other parts of the world catch 'net mania' to the same degree, the nature of internet will change dramatically. While surveys indicate that nearly 90% of web pages currently are in English, that is going to change in the next few years. US-centric websites are being used today by people in other cultures because that's what is available. But as Arabic-language sites offering value become available, for example, Arabic-speaking people will naturally move over to internet services that reflect their cultural identity. Already in India, news and online resources are available from numerous Indian language websites, such as Gujarati *Sandesh*, Tamil *Nakkheeran*, Bengali *Parabaas*, Marathi *Kesari*, and Kannada *Sanjeevani*. In fact, Indian newspapers and magazines went online, almost simultaneously with their Asian and European counterparts. As per the latest count, there are some 60 Indian news publications online. In 1995, there were just 20 newspapers on web, today there are over 4000. Of them 225 are Asian newspapers. An important feature of the online media in India is that majority of the sites are in Indian languages and the English newspaper sites are just eighteen.[12]

Easy Skimming and Scanning

An electronic newspaper facilitates hunting, browsing and/ or grazing. An 'autopilot mode' would flash headlines at a speed set by the reader (who might also set filters, such as 'no sports' and 'new since last Tuesday night'). If something looked interesting, the reader could press a button to stop the flow and read the entire story. At any point, the reader could look something up – a difficult word, a map of a country, a story from last week or last year.[13]

Personalized Context and Atomization

Cyber news allows news consumers to understand the

meaning of the day's events in a personalized context that makes better sense to them than traditional media do now. Since it can build new communities based on shared interests and concerns; and since it has the most unlimited space to offer levels of reportorial depth, texture, and context that are impossible in any other medium – new media can transform journalism.

An example from MSNBC on the internet nicely illustrates the potential. On February 21, 2000, NBC's dateline ran a piece about dangerous roads in America, zeroing in on three particular treacherous thoroughfares. The programme invited viewers to log on to MSNBC site to learn about roads in their community. Those who did so could enter their zip code and, within seconds, based on federal data, find out how many fatal accidents had occurred in that community between 1992 and 1995 and on which roads. Within twelve hours MSNBC logged 68,000 visitors to that feature.[14]

The potential to customize content also means readers may select only what appeals to their narrowest interests. This 'You News' kind of journalism could thus become a force for atomization of the audience for further civic decay. But the optimists do not believe it. Researches for half a century indicate that people use media, new or old, to connect to society, not separate. People go online primarily to connect with the news of their community, whether geographical community or one formed around some other common bond. They use customization features to supplement their general news appetites, following their particular interests in finance, travel, education, environment, or any number of things. So, rather than fracturing society, new media can help to keep us connected. As Dinesh Sharma writes in *Online Journalism Takes Off*, "Of particular interest was the use of the internet by the Chinese diaspora to react to the riots in Indonesia and that of Indian diaspora to the Pokhran nuclear tests and the subsequent economic sanctions imposed by the Clinton administration", it clearly indicates that online journalism helps to connect and build bonds of unity among members of communities scattered over the globe.

Job Opportunities

For the news professionals, online journalism has created more job avenues. A new genre of specialized personnel is emerging in the form of web editors, content providers, web visualizers, web graphic designers, etc. However, this benefit can trickle down to audience only if the intellectuals who wrote for the literati become technology driven, computer friendly and thus, cater to the gentry. The editors have to create newer skills and transform the capability of their news-rooms and editorial chambers to make sense out of both the real and virtual worlds.

Revenue

Most of the newspaper sites in India and abroad are free. In some cases, a few services like archives and other value-added products are charged. But high subscription magazines like the *Economist* and scientific journals like *Science* and *Lancet* are open only to subscribers of their print editions. All the newspaper sites in India are free and their main source of revenue is advertising. The experience so far shows that some of them have become self-sustaining in the short period they have been on the net.

The economics of online publishing are such that you can reach a wider audience with a relatively low investment. The investment is in the form of technical, editorial and software manpower. And once you have the back up of news gathering machinery of the print counterpart, it is easy to generate revenues. Even though the internet rates vary depending on the traffic to the sites as also the positioning of banners/panels on the websites, the cost of advertising on the net is still lower than in the printed paper. Some news sites offer an advertisement banner for as little as Rs. 150 for 1000 impressions.[15] However, rates vary and people have online campaigns that run into lakhs.

The Times of India group ended its first 18 months with a revenue of over rupees two crore on advertising, still as the advertisement rates are much lower than in the print media, the news sites/webzines are impervious to the gagging effect that such inflow of funds can have.

Copyright and Intellectual Property

The biggest concern today is the copyright infringement and protection of intellectual property. Since the internet is in the public domain, there are serious issues regarding copyright on content. Then, there are legal issues like how to deal with defamation on the net. Defamation cases across national boundaries may be a complex issue to resolve since there is no ownership or regulation of the internet as yet. Similarly, inclusion of advertisements of products like liquor and tobacco can be problematic. Drawing the line where the freedom of speech becomes obscenity could be another problem. However, new laws to regulate online journalism in particular and internet as a whole are already on the anvil. The IT bill has already received presidential assent and only needs to be transformed into rules and regulations.

Conservative Attitude

Being technology based, online journalism has to contend with the well entrenched and often irrevocable conservative attitudes of audiences used to the traditional media. The economist Sudip Bannerji says, “Backwardness arises with a negative response to progressive outlook”. It is difficult for technology to permeate into the minds of the people who are reluctant to adopt new innovations and have a negative attitude towards new technology. The need is to make the people more receptive to new technology.

Other factors like high cost of accessing the net, lack of computer literacy, low bandwidth and enormous network traffic can, to a certain extent, decelerate the development of online media in India.

Conclusion

The preceding discussion of the strengths and weaknesses of online journalism from different angles shows that this new genre is here to stay and grow. Notwithstanding the many of the shortcomings attendant on it, online journalism seems to have withstood the test of time reflected as it is in the increasing size of its audience. Besides, it provides a medium where print, audio and video converge and a user-friendly interface satiates the emotional and aesthetic palate of an individual. The ability of web news to cut down the time to get across, to cross the barrier of manual or postal distribution and to bridge the communities separated by geographical boundaries, cannot be overlooked. Many of the negative fallouts of online journalism could be kept in check by the enactment of proper regulations.

NOTES

1. It refers to E.M. Foster's inability to come to terms with the post-Victorian world."
2. *www.ojr.org* (Internet site – Online Journalism Review).
3. Palvik, John V. *The Future of Online Journalism,* The Centre for New Media at Columbia University's Graduate School of Journalism. (www.cjr.org).
4. Sharma, Dinesh C. *Online Journalism Takes Off,* Vidura, Press Institue of India, New Delhi, Vol 35, No.4, Oct-Dec 1998, p. 4.
5. *Ibid.*, p. 8.
6. *www.ojr.org* (Internet site – Online Journalism Review).
7. Sharma, Dinesh C. *op. cit.,* p. 8.
8. *Ibid.*, p. 8.
9. *Ibid.*, p. 8.
10. *www.poynter.org* (Internet site – Online Journalism Seminars).
11. Sharma, Dinesh C. *op. cit.*, p. 5.
12. *Ibid.*, p. 5.
13. Heyer, Mark has described three ways of collecting information in an article in *CD ROM: The New Papyrus* (Internet site *www.cjr.org*) :
    * Hunting is the typical action of looking something up, when a person wants a specific kind of information about a specific topic and conducts a search for it. Hunting takes place in computerized databases today and also in libraries.
    * Browsing is a kind of searching without a specific end, it

is what people do when they scan a daily newspaper, page through a magazine or flip channels on a TV set.

* Grazing is the most passive of the three; Heyer gives an example a TV viewer who turns on the set at seven o'clock and does not move or change stations until he turns the set off at midnight.

14. Palvik, John V. *op. cit.*
15. Katiyar, Arun. Value-Addition is the Key, Vidura, Press Institue of India, New Delhi, Vol. 35, No. 4, Oct-Dec 1998, p. 17.

6
ISSUES IN PRINT AND ELECTRONIC MEDIA

VIR BALA AGGARWAL

Print Media

The press in India continues to be in a state of buoyancy in terms of growth in circulation, number of languages and the multi-city editions in which the newspapers are published. The major challenges before the print media presently are: competition from the electronic media, implementation of right to information, online newspapers and entry of foreign press in the country.

The Indian press enjoys almost complete freedom, subject to certain civil laws—laws of defamation and contempt of court. Freedom of expression is accepted as a core value. Except for the duration of emergency, when pre-censorship was imposed and some of the journalists had to undergo harrowing experience, the Indian press has been able to maintain its freedom. Whenever, there was a threat to freedom of press, legislative or otherwise, the journalists came out as one man and one community to defend challenge to the freedom of expression.

The Press Council of India (PCI) intervenes and adjudicates complaints from the public, mostly against the wrong doings or excesses of individual journalists or the newspapers; but it has only advisory authority. The PCI has, however, been making efforts to evolve a code of conduct for journalists, and also scrutinise the role of press in a national crisis situation; like the demolition of Babri Masjid.

TABLE 6.1 : Number of Newspapers in 1999 (Language and Periodicity-wise)

Languages	*Dailies*	*Tri/Bi-Weeklies*	*Weeklies*	*Fortnightlies*	*Monthlies*	*Quarterlies Halfyearlies*	*Bi-monthlies*	*Annuals*	*Total*
English	371	30	881	671	2,734	1,210	771	162	6,830
Hindi	2,305	125	9,608	2,878	3,180	589	185	33	18,903
Assamese	15	3	75	38	59	12	10	1	213
Bengali	99	14	594	494	681	458	169	17	2,526
Gujarati	118	11	776	182	492	58	47	14	1,698
Kannada	314	6	354	231	589	44	19	4	1,561
Kashmiri	0	0	1	0	0	0	0	0	1
Konkani	1	0	3	1	1	0	0	0	6
Malayalam	213	6	174	156	732	57	27	8	1,373
Manipuri	14	0	6	5	10	6	3	0	44
Marathi	346	20	1,108	189	504	110	41	113	2,431
Nepali	3	2	20	6	8	16	5	0	60
Oriya	71	2	142	83	267	88	23	4	680
Punjabi	107	15	350	89	237	32	18	1	849
Sanskrit	3	0	8	4	16	15	6	0	52
Sindhi	11	0	38	11	35	8	2	0	105
Tamil	352	43	393	227	786	32	22	8	1,863
Telugu	151	3	245	187	480	26	12	2	1,106
Urdu	519	20	1,317	361	506	60	17	3	2,803
Bilingual	73	19	593	334	1,148	336	142	34	2,679
Multilingual	17	4	103	63	208	67	34	12	508
Others	54	14	83	30	123	49	11	0	364
Total	5,157	337	16,872	6,240	12,796	3,273	1,564	416	46,655

Source: India 2001.

During the nineties the press had to face increasing challenge from the satellite television channels. Several publishing houses established TV divisions, with the *India Today* group becoming quite successful with its news programmes. During mid-1995, TV channels became a growth industry and several senior journalists joined TV journalism, which offered better packages and instant visibility. While TV offered opportunity to give instantaneous news — news as it was breaking, particularly during the Kargil conflict and the recent parliamentary elections; press gave background briefing and analysis to the news events. The press has also started giving greater coverage to subjects like arts, science and technology and law as well as to societal concerns like literacy, education and environment.

The rapid technological change, which the print media is adapting to survive, has brought about far-reaching changes in the contemporary media scenario. The leading newspapers are taking to online journalism in a big way. Commenting on the latest developments in the field, a recent business journal (*Business World*, 15 May 2000) wrote: The onslaught of technology is changing the dynamics of news delivery too. Newspapers, once the medium for breaking news, relinquished that role to television. The Internet could take that over. Crudely, the new media ecosystem could look like this: the Net will break news, TV will do follow ups and live coverage and newspapers will end up doing analyses. Some of this may already be happening. At *The Washington Post*, for instance, newspaper reporters file crisp, shorter articles for the web and file bigger articles for the newspaper.

Several print media organisations—*The Hindu*, *Times of India* and *India Today* and others have been developing comprehensive websites of their own, which regularly cover interviews, chat shows, business and economy news, life styles and entertainment. In fact online journalism is creating more opportunities of employment and advancement for the print media journalists and the competition to retain the best journalists in the print media is becoming really sharp.

Right to Information

The initiative in this regard, taken by the *Mazdoor, Kisan Shakti Sangathan* (MKSS) since 1990 to mobilise local opinion received support from several organisations and voluntary bodies including PII, PCI, PUCL and individuals. Draft bills prepared by PCI, and the Working Group set up at the National Institute of Rural Development, Hyderabad (September 1997) elicited wide spread support successfully culminated in government's resolve in bringing right to information bill to the parliament.

Entry of Foreign Newspapers in India

The entry of foreign newspapers in India is an issue that has polarised the media community, with both the protagonists and the opponents speaking on the move with almost religious fervour. Those favouring the move consider the step as the logical outcome of the on-going process of liberalisation, whereas those opposing advise caution against going blind folded into an unknown area and cite the 1955 cabinet decision disallowing such entry as sacrosanct. The successive governments had categorically decided to stand by the 1955 cabinet decision. The issue was debated at several fora including institutions like Editor's Guild, professional bodies of journalists and editors.

Unlike the Indian press, the foreign newspapers are not expected to have any concern for our culture, ethos or traditions. The cultural and moral fallout of the entry of the foreign newspapers would be far more serious than fallout of the advent of Satellite T.V. in the country where the print media still has greater influence than the electronic media.

At present many western countries have severe restrictions against foreign ownership of the print media. Unless there is a worldwide level playing field, foreign equity will introduce another inequity in this sensitive area.

Ruling out the opening of print media to foreign investors, the Information and Broadcasting Minister said recently that political consensus uniform across the board was against any such proposal and the consensus was (*Times of India*, 30.3.2000).

Electronic Media

The recent years have witnessed exponential growth in the media industry, particularly in electronic and satellite communication, and rapid advances in communication technology. Massive growth of television has been primarily due to operationalisation of INSAT satellite system in 1982, the live coverage of the Gulf war by CNN in 1991; which led to the proliferation of transnational foreign satellite programmes. Another way of looking at the television expansion in the country is: the reach of Doordarshan in 1998 increased to 86 per cent of population as against 25 per cent in 1980; the number of programme production centres has gone up from 10 to 45 during the same period. The number of programmes produced by Doordarshan catering to the specific needs of languages and regions has also substantially increased; as also the number of TV households from 6.8 million in 1985 to 63.2 million cable and satellite households in the country.

In a case study 'TV Contents in Asia: More Waste or Substance', S.R. Joshi says: But the overall major thrust is one of entertainment of soap opera kind. Quite a few of the Indian language channels depend on the Indian feature film industry for providing this entertainment. This includes both showing of feature films as well as feature film based programmes like songs and dances, etc. The Training and Development Communication Channel (TDCC) of ISRO is using television for Training Panchyati Raj elected representatives; Aanganwadi workers, primary school teachers, mid-wives, etc. This network-TDCC is spreading out to several States and distance education agencies like Indira Gandhi National Open University (IGNOU), All India Management Association, NGO's like Self-Employed Women's Association (SEWA) and

Ahmedabad Women's Action Group (AWAG). However, there is greater need to reorient TV programmes, also to make use of non-dominant forms of communication to respond to development needs of the target groups. Likewise the possibility of multi-media technology including Internet to harness the requirements of development objectives has yet to be explored in the right earnest.

Television

Today TV is no longer an urban phenomenon. Its penetration, in the sub-urban and mofussil areas, and even in villages, is not considered a big deal any longer. There has, in fact, been a virtual paradigm shift from state monopoly of electronic media to virtual *laissez faire*; from the position of monopoly national broadcaster to one of the players is indeed a metamorphosis in the media landscape in the country.

TABLE 16.2 : Terrestrial Coverage

	No. of Transmitters	*Percentage of Population Covered*
1982	19	25.7
1987	197	70.3
1992	531	81.1
1997	868	87.1
1999	1,000	87.6
2003	1,400	93.0*

* Proposed.

Programme Content
DD-1 : National
(Hours per Week)

	1985 (30 hrs)	*1990 (50 hrs)*	*1995 (80 hrs)*	*1999 (105 hrs)*
News & Current Affairs (Hindi & English)	5	10	15	25
Hindi Film Based	5	7	12	10
Hindi Serials	5	8	20	30
Education	7	12	15	12
Sports	1	4	12	15
Culture	3	3	1	1
Other Indian Languages	—	4	2	2
Others	4	2	3	5

Satellite Channels

General Entertainment	Hindi :	Zee, Home, Sony, Star Plus
	Tamil :	Sun, Raj, Vijay
	Telugu :	Enadu, Gemini
	Kannada :	Uday
	Malayalam :	Asianet, Surya
Thematic Channels	Movies :	Zee Cinema, Star Movies, TNT
	Sports :	Star Sports, ESPN
	Children :	Cartoon Network
	News :	BBC World, CNN, TVI, Zee India, Star
	Music :	Channel V, MTV
	Nature :	Discovery, National Geographic

Source for the Tables: B.S. Chandrasekhar - *More Channels: More Choice, More Quality* (2000).

From Regional Languages to Local Dialects

After the boom in regional channels in the domestic television industry, it is now turn of sub-regional channels like Rajasthani, Bihari and Sindhi. In an interview the *Times of India* (15.7.2000) the Chief Executive Officer of a media company says : It is an unexplored belt. We see a potential business in these channels. The numbers of cable connections in the country is to increase because of these new regional channels. Regional channels are the fastest growing segment in broadcasting. Southern market is already overcrowded. In 8-10 months at least 20 more satellite channels would begin to beam into India in addition to existing 60 channels.

Public Service Broadcasting

In the contemporary political, economic and cultural scenario, the policy makers in all countries have allowed radio and television to become a marketing vehicle rather than a cultural element. There will continue to be obvious need for a kind of television that pays attention to cultural, social, educational and economic needs of the people. The basic issue confronting us in the years ahead is : Whether broadcasting will be considered mainly as an industry turning out a commercial "product" and associated totally with marketing or will it be first of all an institution to permit access to culture, knowledge and enlightened entertainment for all the people, or in other words should broadcasting be devoted to education and other public services or strictly to business of entertainment. In the above context public service broadcasting becomes the imperative need of our times.

The national broadcasters should bear the responsibility to offer a high quality public service broadcasting that informs, educates and entertains the people. Adequate care should be taken to enable the setting up of non-commercial broadcasting stations to be run by universities, educational institutions, panchayats/local bodies, State governments, etc. Prasar Bharati as the inheritor of the great tradition should be the quintessential public service broadcaster. This is not to suggest that private broadcasters have no role to play in this sphere. Indeed, the private operators should have an obligation to put out programmes devoted to socially relevant themes and earmark certain slots for the purpose.

The public service broadcasting manifesto, propounded by the first Director General of BBC, John Reith: The service must not be used for entertainment purposes alone. Broadcasting has a responsibility to bring into the greatest possible number of homes in the fullest degree all that was best in every department of human knowledge endeavour and achievement. The preservation of high moral tone and the avoidance of the vulgar were of paramount importance. Broadcasting should give lead to public taste rather than pander to it.

On the threshold of the millennium, India, the Indian society and the Indian media are all in transition. The trends that the media is witnessing today are bound to gather strength; while some others are bound to emerge in the wake of rapid technological innovations and developments.

The dramatic emergence of information societies has led to a revolution in communication in the shape of multimedia systems and the spectacular expansion of information technology networks, including internet. The impact of the expansion of Internet is still limited in developing countries, owing to the relatively small number of people with the necessary technology know-how. Every thing suggests that an unstoppable revolution is in progress which will make it possible to transmit and ever increasing mass of information in shorter span of time. At the same time, thanks to the falling cost of equipment, the new technologies are steadily finding their way into every aspect of work. This is where the opportunity lies for the media in the new millennium. And of course the challenge would be how to harness the potential of media for the nation building and national development.

REFERENCE

India 2001, Publications Division. Ministry of Information and Broadcasting, Government of India.

MEDIA AND DEVELOPMENT

7
DEVELOPMENT
Global Civil Religion

V. S. GUPTA

Development—its evolution and changing perceptions during the last half a century has had a fascinating history. It has been open to a large number of definitions, connotations and interpretations. The vastness of the canvas it encompasses within its ambit is truly amazing—from economic and social development to human resource development and now development as a human right. In its broadest sense development tends to be an umbrella under which several phenomena-varying from human to spiritual development, economic and community development, as well as technological development have become inter-related. Development has been the dominant theme of the international discourse in the decades following the Second World War. It has been a search rather than an achieved goal and the goal continues into the millennium and beyond.

Right to Development

Today human rights include right to development. Achieving development is no longer what the state may opt to "do". It is now the primary responsibility of the government to create national and international conditions favourable to the realization of the right to development. The Declaration on the right to development, which was adopted by the General Assembly of the United Nations on 4 December 1986 is particularly significant for its importance to the developing countries. The Declaration states that the human person is the central subject of development and should be the active participant and beneficiary of the right to development. Article 8 in particular says : The States should undertake, at the national level, all necessary measures for the realization of the right to development and shall ensure, *inter alia*, equality of opportunity for all in their access to basic resources—education, health services, food, housing, employment and the fair distribution of income. Effective measures should be undertaken to ensure that women have an active role in the development process.

Promotion and protection of human rights in a plural society under a democratic framework require sustained efforts of the government and non-government organizations at different levels. An independent judiciary and vigilant media are essential institutions to safeguard people's rights.

Apart from the right to development, another basic, and equally significant entitlement to human survival is right to communicate. Some governments, notably the United States, have included communication right as a basic right for their citizens. The Universal Declaration of Human Rights under Article 19 states: Every one has the right to freedom of opinion and expression. This right includes freedom to hold opinions without interference and to seek, receive and impart information and ideas through any media and regardless of frontiers. As a result the right to information and communication is receiving greater attention in the contemporary affairs.

Development has become global "civil religion" during the past more than 40 years—a battle cry for all nations—rich or poor, strong or weak. It is a long and complex evolutionary process—more a process of social change rather than merely generation and accumulation of economic resources. Development thinking has evolved into a broad spectrum realization that it must move beyond economic growth to include important social goals—reduced poverty, improved quality of life, enhanced opportunities for better education and health, and more. Experience has also taught that sustainable progress towards these goals requires integrated implementation and must be firmly anchored in processes that are open, participatory and inclusive.

Development in order to be impactive and durable, has to be sustainable. The *World Development Report* 1999/2000, *Entering the 21st Century* says : Sustainable development has many objectives. Raising per capita incomes is only one among many such objectives. Improving quality of life involves more specific goals : better health services and educational opportunities, greater participation in public life, a clean environment, intergenerational equity and more. Outcomes of policies based on consensual, participatory and transparent processes are more easily sustained. Institutions of good governance that employ such processes are critical for development and should encompass partnership among all elements of civil society.

The development issue is characterised by its scale and magnitude. It is perceived more and more to be with broad masses of people—the development tide is turning more and more to favour the people—for instance now we have goals like *Education for All*, *Health for All*. However, the universalistic trend is riven by a development gap between advanced and poor countries. The development agenda is bypassing the poorer nations.

There has, however, been a refreshing rethinking and realisation that single-thrust industrialization has created deprivation and marginalization of children, women and the depressed poor. This rethinking is crystallised in the expression of regret on the part of Professor Tinbergon, who propounded the concept of GNP as a measure of progress. The use of GNP is steering the society with a wrong compass. GNP gives, imperfectly and somewhat deceptively, a measure of the aggregate value of national goods and services. It conceals the distribution of wealth and gives a deceptive picture of social health. Since the computation of GNP is not accompanied by a computation of Gross Destruction of Basic Resources (GDBR)—soil degradation, pollution of water and the atmosphere, depletion of mineral resources, the entry of toxic wastes in the food chain, and so on—it is a faulty indicator of economic health.

Inspite of massive investments in the rural development and poverty alleviation programmes the benefits have not percolated down to the poor and the intended beneficiaries. Several factors have been responsible for such a situation : the existing power structure of village institutions such as panchayats and cooperative societies which are captured by the rich and the politically influential people: centralised planning process emanating from the union government and lack of awareness about the development programmes and projects available. It is now being increasingly realised that although we have a functioning democratic government in our country, people have hardly any role in shaping their destinies at various levels which has severely affected the quality of governance in the country. The planning is mostly Delhi-centric; and the planning process concentrated in the offices of the central government and the Planning Commission. There have not been many people-sponsored and village-sponsored schemes.

There has been repeated criticism of the whole concept of development and the way the task of planned development was initiated and implemented. There has been greater realization that the economic betterment of the poor sections cannot be achieved without social transformation involving structural changes, educational development, growth in awareness and change in outlook, motivation and attitudes. Social change can be achieved through greater participation of the poor by electing them to the grassroot level institutions. The Seventh Five Year Plan (1985-90) document says : Improvement of literacy and education, both through formal and non-formal means, and the imaginative use of the mass media for communicating useful information and knowledge as well as for changing the outlook of the people by instilling in them the egalitarian spirit, the urge for and confidence in achieving self betterment through cooperative endeavour, are essential for setting up the process of socio-economic transformation. It is now being frequently admitted that due to deficiencies noticed in the implementation of plan projects, illiteracy and lack of awareness on the part of beneficiaries, and chain of intermediaries, on the other hand, only a small portion of the intended outlay reaches the actual recipients.

Communication and Development

Likewise our understanding of role and process of communication in development has also witnessed paradigm shift. Initially the Western communication scholars thought that mass communication, particularly radio could overcome barrier to illiteracy and distance and change the tradition based consciousness of the Third World peasants who stood in the way of modernization. The new development communication perspective underlines community orientation, community radio, community listening groups, self management and self reliance, voluntary action and right to participate. It is increasingly stressed that knowledge, experience and view point of local people be given due consideration before decisions are arrived at. The beneficiaries of the development programmes be not considered as passive recipients, they should rather be taken as stake holders in the success of development process.

Another interesting and related aspect is that communication technology itself has taken a quantum leap in the past decade. The focus has shifted from development support communication to computerization and digitalization; from rural communication to satellite communication. Information has become infotainment and editorial has become advertorial—clearly signifying shift of emphasis from information and journalism to entertainment and advertisement. Sometimes it appears that in the new era of technology, deregulation and commercialization, and the sway of market forces, the development dialogue has lost its relevance. This is the experience of the author after participating in a number of seminars in South East Asian countries and also in the metropolitan towns in India.

However, winds of change are blowing over all NGOs working with rural communities. In Danta Ramgarh tehsil of Sikar district in Rajasthan an NGO has offered for public scrutiny documents of financial expenditure incurred in implementing its programmes during the ten years of its existence. A 'transparency *mela*' organised by the NGO in this tiny village took the people of the area by a pleasant surprise. SARA (Social Action for Rural Advancement) is engaged in works relating to rural development, literacy, education, health care, environment protection, afforestation, drinking water and watershed development. The SARA director was unambiguous about the need for maintaining transparency in the voluntary sector, when we never lag behind in demanding the right to information about the government activities and decisions, it is pious duty to ensure our own accountability to the people among whom we are working.—*Grassroots* Vol. 1, No. 4; August 1999, reporting the human condition.

Development and Public Activism

Public activism is considered a legitimate tool for accelerating social and human development. India's democratic institutions—electoral process, news media, village panchayats provide potential bases for public action in siezing opportunities for social and economic development. While analysing the reasons for the frequent occurrence of famines in China, Sen and Dreze point out that the Chinese government did not wake up to the nature and magnitude of the calamity for quite a long time and the disastrous policies were not substantially revised for three years, while the famine raged on because of the informational failure. The informational failure, linked to controlled press, duped not only the public in suppressing information about the famine, but the government was also deluded as well. Whereas in a democratic country, no substantial famine has ever occurred because the government which has to deal with opposition parties, face condemnation from public media, and to go to polls on a regular basis, cannot afford not to take prompt action to avert threatening famine.[1]

The SEWA (Self-Employed Women's Association) led by the eminent social activist, Ela Bhatt has shown the way by using video technology for articulating grievances of women construction workers, vegetable sellers and other such self-employed women who had no forum for collective social action. Protesting against the municipal action of removing the vegetable sellers from their traditional work place on the Manekchowk of Ahmedabad, these women videotaped their protest movement, their agitating mood and their determination to resist the decision of Municipal Committee to remove them from there. The videotaped meetings and agitation convinced the municipal authorities of the apprehensions and grievances of the women workers. The authorities thereafter decided to drop their plan of shifting them from their traditional work place.

Addressing a professional body of communication experts in June 1993, the Minister for Information and Broadcasting said that programmes on socio-economic developmental issues produced by All India Radio and Doordarshan had failed to fascinate listeners and viewers. He observed : No matter the amount of money spent or the time allotted to the media some of the programmes are dull and do not have any imagination or concern at the quality of radio and TV programmes on developmental issues. As various types of programmes oriented on socio-economic development issues are not imaginative and fascinating, the listener or the viewer simply turns off the knob, as a result the developmental measures do not percolate to the people.

This desperate situation can be remedied only through more training opportunities for media professionals about environment, biodiversity, micro credit system being implemented by organisations like Grameen Bank, and TAMBULI in the Philippines, which is the call name of a series of community radio stations. Likewise NGO's video strategy, widely involving rural people in Bangladesh, Nepal, Sri Lanka, India has also been effective in creating an environment of participation.

Public Service Broadcasting

In the contemporary political, economic and cultural scenario, where policy makers in all countries have allowed radio and television to become a marketing vehicle rather than a cultural element; there will continue to be obvious need for a kind of television that pays attention to cultural, social, educational and economic needs of the people. The basic issue confronting us in the years ahead is : Whether broadcasting will be considered mainly as an industry turning out a commercial "product" and associated totally with marketing or will it be first of all an institution to permit access to culture, knowledge and enlightened entertainment for all the people, or in other words should broadcasting be devoted to education and other public services or strictly to business. In the above context public service broadcasting becomes the imperative need of our times.

The Consultative Committee recommended : The national broadcasters should bear the responsibility to offer a high quality public service broadcasting that informs, educates and entertains the people. Adequate care should be taken to enable the setting up of non-commercial broadcasting stations to be run by universities, educational institutions, panchayats/local bodies, State governments, etc. Likewise, the Working Group (Sengupta Committee) said : This Group believes that Prasar Bharati as the inheritor of the great tradition should be the quintessential public service broadcaster. This is not to suggest that private broadcasters have no role to play in this sphere. Indeed, the private operators should have an obligation to put out programmes devoted to socially relevant themes and earmark certain slots for the purpose. The public service broadcasting manifesto, propounded by the first Director General of BBC, John Reith says :

> The service must not be used for entertainment purposes alone. Broadcasting has a responsibility to bring into the greatest possible number of homes in the fullest degree all that was best in every department of human knowledge, endeavour and achievement. The preservation of high moral tone, the avoidance of the vulgar and the hurtful was of paramount importance. Broadcasting should give lead to public taste rather than pander to it.

At times, these views of Reith have been criticised as paternalistic. Whereas there has been a large body of support for the ethos of public service broadcasting, it has been showing signs of crisis in this era of deregulation and commercialization. It would of course be readily accepted that dangers of deregulated system must be encountered by putting in place suitable measures.

Policy Formulation and Civil Society Organisations

A multitude of players outside of the government sector grassroot organisations, trade unions, universities, non profit foundations, user groups and non-governmental organisations influence public performance. Among the things they can hold local governments and civic bodies accountable. Such groups known collectively as "civil society", can also aid local administration in search for more responsive and effective governance.

In India, and more so at the international level, the increasing role of non-governmental organisations, voluntary bodies and other organs of the civil society in advocacy and policy formulation has introduced a new element in democratic governance. In the contemporary society policy formulation is not left to governments alone. In the Foreword to a book *Public Policy, Analysis and Design*, the eminent Indian diplomat, economist and educational administrator, A.M. Khusro says : Policy need not be made by governments only, but in this country policy has been made almost wholly by governments. It may be because other segments and sectors—the commercial sector and the social sector—have been weak and are in the throes of a slow developmental process, they will acquire a degree of resilience and a policy making capability later. But to begin with they were weak and therefore, it fell to the lot of Central and State governments to make policies and programmes during the last 40 years. There are NGOs like Policy Initiatives or Policy Alternatives, etc. and there are associations of industry and trade. Many people in the private sector of industry and trade, the cooperative sector, the NGO sector, the social sector and intellectual sector, are beginning to think of many policy areas and it is certain that their role will increase with time.

The special issue of *Development Dialogue*, published by Dag Hammarskjold Foundation devotes one paper to the responsibilities of civil society organisations. In the systems analysis, the paper makes fascinating study : In eighties the First System comprised of princes (the politicians and the governments); while the second position fell to merchants (now transnational enterprises). Today the reality is otherwise. In several countries including USA, UK, Canada, Australia and Japan, the merchants dictate to the princes. Globalisation has become a corporate mantra mouthed by politicians. It is widely known that US corporations do not act for the benefit of US economy. The Second System is under attack from CSOs, which constitute the Third System. Increasingly the disenchanted sectors of civil society are asking—Why governments who cannot deliver services should be permitted to set policies. In any future dispensation CSOs will be forced to take a more aggressive policy role.

We may recall that it is because of the sustained hard work put in by organisations like NBA that today even the World Bank has agreed to revisit the claims of big dams and irrigation projects. It is only because of the critical scrutiny of the CSOs that the role of international conferences like the Earth Summit and the Beijing Conference are being evaluated for concrete results.

Erosion of rights is one area where challenge to human dignity is the greatest. CSOs are increasingly looking to constitutional and legal remedies for safeguarding human rights mechanisms to counter the force of World Trade Organisation (see the devastating effect with which the recent WTO conference in US was confronted by NGOs and VOs.). The invocation of human rights (which would include freedom of expression, of the press, right to development, political opinion and education) draws together a broad spectrum of civil society and holds real promise of success.

We have seen how several CSOs have made effective intervention regarding Freedom of Information Act. Another such no profit trust *Voices* has been working as a communication resource and advocacy group. The Bangalore-based media NGO, *Voices*, has been spearheading a movement to examine issues relating to democratisation in media, the right to communicate and access to information and communication technologies particularly by the economically and socially deprived. Its journal *Voices* provides a forum to a vast cross-section of the media academics and scholars, working in the voluntary and social sectors and all others interested in working for change in the society.

The Indian press by far the freest press in South Asia, pluralistic, multi-lingual, continues to be largely urban-oriented. More so the metropolitan press; and the newspapers coming out from the national capital are Delhi centric. The press in English language is elitist geared to the commercial culture, obsessed with garnering the maximum share of advertising revenue. Issues concerning rural development are not given adequate coverage.

India—with its vast population of one billion people—with seventy per cent living in rural areas severely need more such initiatives. Let it not be said of its planners, writers and communication experts that they showed no propensity to solve the problems such as alleviation of poverty, illiteracy and lack of guidance and sharing of development experience with other sections of society to make development an all-encompassing and participatory process. Development has to be an engrossing passion with the people of the country. It is simply too important a mission to be left to planners and government administrators alone. If we could make development a people-oriented movement we would have taken the first concrete and constructive step in the new millennium.

NOTE

1. One of the first papers of the author—Development Communication—An Emerging Concept—appeared in *Vidura* in 1979. Since then there has been a constant endeavour to understand and reflect on various aspects of development policy, its implementation, deficiencies, as well as how the media of communication could be harnessed to make development more meaningful and relevant to the intended beneficiaries.

REFERENCES

Asian Mass Communication Research and Information Centre (1996). *Opening Windows—Issues in Communication*, Singapore.

David McQueen (1998). *Television—A Media Students Guide*, Arnold, London.

Development Dialogue (1996). 1-2; Dag Hammarskjold Foundation, Uppsala.

Entering the 21st Century—World Development Report. 1999/2000, The World Bank Washington.

Grassroots (1999). Reporting the human condition (1-7) Press Institute of India, New Delhi.

Gupta, V.S. (1996). Media Strategies for Rural Development. In : *Kurukshetra*, Vol. XLIV, No. 4-5.

Gupta, V.S. (1995). *Third Revolution in Indian Perspective—Contemporary Issues and Themes in Communication.*

Gupta, V.S. (1999). *Communication Technology, Media Policy and National Development.*

Gupta, V.S. and Vir Bala Aggarwal (1996). *Media Policy and Nation Building—Select Issues and Themes.*

Knowledge for Development, World Development Report 1998/99, The World Bank, Washington.

Learning : The Treasure Within (1996). Report to UNESCO of the

International Commission on Education for the Twentyfirst Century, UNESCO, Paris.

Public Service Broadcasting (1997). *The Challenge of the Twenty-first Century*—UNESCO.

Voices (1995). Changing with Radio; Vol. III, No. 3, Bangalore.

Voices (1997). Consultation on Media Policy and Community Radio. Workshop Report, Bangalore.

8

MEDIA AND RURAL POVERTY ALLEVIATION PROGRAMMES

M.M. GOEL

In this paper an attempt has been made to justify the role of a journalist in a situation where rural poverty alleviation programmes are in jeopardy. In fact, the press coverage of the rural development issues including poverty alleviation programmes is necessary but not sufficient unless a journalist is treated as an input in the strict sense of economics and calls for making development communication effective and result oriented. This calls for a media strategy for rural development, which suits the beneficiaries and is relevant for them and uses every opportunity to ensure their participation—consultation, cooperation and effective mobilization. Truly, rural press can prove to be a catalyst change and progress of the rural people by understanding, analysing and highlighting the issues concerning one and all. Of course, there is a need of understanding constraints of a journalist in rural development reporting and makes a case for encouragement and motivation through National Awards for them.

The present rural development programmes includes Swaranjayanti Gram Swarozgar Yojana (SGSY)—a single self-employment programme since April 1999 restructured from IRDP, TRYSEM, DWCRA and MWS with the objective of focussed approach to poverty alleviation, capitalizing advantages of group lending and overcoming the problems associated with multiplicity of programmes for below poverty line (BPL) families and is funded by Centre and State Governments in the ratio of 75 : 25.

Jawahar Gram Samridhi Yojana (JGSY)—a wage employment programme since April 1999 restructured from JRY for creation of demand driven village infrastructure including durable assets at the village level to enable the rural poor to increase the opportunities for sustained employment families. Employment Assurance Scheme since October 2, 1999 have been restructured as a single wage employment programme from April 1999 with a fixed annual outlay and is being implemented presently in 5448 rural blocks through Zila Parishad for creating additional wage employment for BPL people.

To look ahead for higher growth of Indian economy, we need to ensure at least 4% average annual growth rate of agricultural and allied activities which calls for policy framework to encourage higher investment in rural assets and channel public expenditure towards supportive infrastructure including rural roads, irrigation, agricultural research and extension services and soil conservation. The existing restrictions on the movement of agricultural produce between States should be eliminated so that farmer can be benefited from a single national market. A concerted effort needs to be made to revamp the system of rural credit to put it on firmer footing.

It needs to be noted that the economic cost of the FCI incurred for procurement, storage, distribution, driage and wastage of foodgrains have been rising in recent years and are now much above the free market prices and is a cause of concern and if not checked, it may keep on rising the burden of food subsidy. This calls for highlighting the measures to economize on the cost by FCI.

To remove rural poverty we will have to check corruption in-built in poverty alleviation programmes. Corruption starts from the recruitment of manpower with bribe and needs to be recognized as key development issue. It is not only a social problem but is an economic offence of highest order. Corruption in India is the social cost of democracy and may prove to be a potential threat to its very survial. It needs to be analysed in a comprehensive socio-economic context. It is a well-identified factor of socio-economic inequalities in India, which are increasing day by day. Corruption in India has assumed alarming proportions and has become the serious disease of cancer for the whole nation.

Where do the allocated funds by the Central Government to the State Governments for rural development go? The reply to this question is well known. It is the same reply, which was given by late Shri Rajiv Gandhi, the former Prime Minister. He was of the well considered opinion that out of the big amount only fifteen per cent reaches the needy in the rural areas and the rest of 85 per cent is cornered by the corrupt intermediaries.

It is interesting to note that the truth of corruption in administrative machinery which was accepted at the level of the Prime Minister late Shri Rajiv Gandhi. By this we can safely conclude that the problem of corruption is so universalized that it is difficult to estimate its extent. If at all this problem has emerged as a sensitive issue in the last decade, we can note with certainty that if the amount of fifteen per cent of rural development funds used to reach the ultimate beneficiary during the times of Rajiv Gandhi, it might be only ten percent now. There is no authentic and objective documentation of crime and corruption (CC) history of India. Are we not guilty of keeping our people in dark? The CC activities are increasing with an alarming rate in India for which, to some extent, our information technology is contributing considerably. The prohibition era in Haryana with CC of all kinds is the most authentic proof of this reality.

Dr. Ajit Kumar Sinha (1999) is right in observing that the State and the society as a whole suffer from the activities of the criminals organised as crime syndicates and is emerging as a major economic power to become a law unto themselves. He is right in making a case for identifying measures to break the vicious circles of crime as a pre-condition of development for which we have to arouse mass consciousness.

It needs to be noted carefully from 'the anatomy of

corruption' by Shri S.L. Sharma (2000) that the decline of moral and social values and the disconcerting trend of loss of fear of law provide a conducive climate for the growth of CC. It has to be understood that CC are flourishing under conditions of scarcity and shortage of goods and services; heavy regulations, red tape and procedural delay; lack of transparency and accountability; low and inadequate salaries; advertent or inadvertent violations of rules; and above all, culture of greed and consumerism.

According to Shri M.G. Devasahayam (2000) in India there are endless stories of starvation, pollution, drought, death and destruction caused by corruption in the Government and business that is going on unabated. He noted that despite spending thousands of crores of rupees in the last five decades large part of India are still without safe drinking water, quality power and motorable roads, it is in large measure due to corruption. He quoted recent cases of corruption unearthed in the handling of Orissa's cyclone and Gujarat's drought which highlight the extent to which government officials in India have been brutalized by this despicable venom! According to him there are two sides of corruption: demand and supply. Unless both sides are tackled simultaneously with equal vehemence, not much can be done to root out this cancer which has already eaten up much of the vitals of Indian society and economy. As of now, Indian legal, judicial, vigilance and investigative systems are oriented mainly to grapple with demand side corruption, virtually leaving out the supply side from its ambit.

It needs to be noted that considerable amount of money is being sanctioned by the Central Government for the needy in rural areas every year but remains under utilized by the State Governments and is being returned back to the Central Government. On the other hand, State Governments like Trade Union's leader continue demanding more funds from the Central Government. This has led to increase the coefficients of distrust between the Centre and the State.

Let us have a look at the statistics from Indira Awas Yojana for poor people during 1998-99. The State Governments have utilized 65 per cent of the allocated funds by the Centre. In Bihar, Haryana, Himachal Pradesh, Madhya Pradesh, Manipur, Uttar Pradesh, Andaman and Nicobar the funds utilized are only 60 per cent. The utilization under this programme varies between 11.50 per cent to 48.40 per cent in Arunachal Pradesh, Assam, J&K, Meghalaya, Nagaland and West Bengal. It needs to be noted carefully that all these States are suffering from acute poverty. This observed pattern of utilization of funds, to some extent, is because of the in-built corruption deep rooted in our system at various levels.

One of the fine examples of CC in Integrated Rural Development Programme is the pattern of purchasing buffalo by the poor in rural areas. A poor man had a buffalo but he needed money to get his daughter married for which there were no provision under the schemes. At the instance of the officials he was asked to get loan for a buffalo (he already possessed). He got the loan, of course, by bribing the so called seller of the buffalo who gave the certificate of sale duly verified by the village officials, bank authorities and several others. All this in-built corruption could have been avoided had there been a provision of getting the loan for the marriage of the daughter. Truly, it is an economic offence on the part of the administrative machinery to increase the deprivation of this kind among the poorest of the poors.

The deep rooted corruption in public distribution system is evident from the statement of Union Minister of Consumer Affairs and Public Distribution, Mr. Shanta Kumar at Dharamsala on June 25, 2000 that a Rs. five crore foodgrains consignment sent to North-East five years ago was yet to reach there. No action was taken against the erring officials.

Why are most of the rural Indians poor?

It is the poverty of governance, which is responsible for the messy state of affairs. It is the poverty of ideas at the helm of affairs. And more than that, it is the poverty of will and determination to implement those innovative ideas which would benefit the rural poor. Rather it has facilitated the operation of 'might is right' to the detriment of the rule of law. That the innocent fear the police more than the criminals is no hyperbole. Poverty-absolute, relative, primary, secondary, hydrological or of any kind is demoralizing for every one. It is true that if a free society cannot help the many that are poor, it cannot save the few who are rich.

To my mind, the reduced working life is the root cause of CC in India. Theoretically the working life starts at 18—the age of entry in employment and continues up to the retirement age of 60, providing sufficient time of 42 years to fulfil the responsibilities and liabilities of an individual. But, practically, due to many well identified factors such as increased number of years for educational qualifications, unemployment, incidence of disease, accidents it is not possible to start the working life at the age of 18. An average Indian, in the present circumstances, is able to get the employment at the age of 30 leading to reduced working life required for fulfilling all the obligation at family, neighbourhood, relative and society levels. This leads to accept and adopt CC as a way of life for an individual. There is a strong correlation between CC and reduced working life as is evident from the fact that our political leaders who have smaller working lives are more corrupt.

We need to recognize that the *status quo* on CC has only brought misery without progress. In a situation like this there is an urgent need for the media to step in a big way. Diffusion of knowledge about CC by media can bring in feeling of fear among the potential criminals. It will create an atmosphere of honesty all around. As opinion makers and public ambassadors, the media can bring a revolution in India. What it reports with honesty of purpose is accepted by the masses. The media, thus, fulfils the role of informant and watchdog in the interest of masses. It is imperative that the media persons understand the role they have to play in making India CC free. It is, they who can create elusive environment in which trust begets trust.

As CC, an act of human behaviour, cannot be controlled by criminal law. It should be dealt with human approach to remove behavioural pollution among criminals and corrupt people so that they can accept honesty in times to come. To propagate the dictum, 'Honesty is the best policy' we have to identify the role models such as Azina Hasham Premji, who built the massive Wipro Corporation by proving that honesty pays and it is possible to be a clean person in India and yet build a company of $20 billion.

The criminals of various kinds in India are insensitive to social stigma and do not admit their guilt. They fail to confess their crime publicly. They need to be made guilt conscious by creating a culture which is conducive for this task to be undertaken at all levels. To make India CC free, media needs to tell people to distinguish between the merits and demerits of an honest vis-a-vis corrupt and criminal. They need to be made fully equipped to contribute towards the society. To remove CC in rural development programmes in India we need to replace target oriented approach by result oriented approach. There is need of replacing *post mortem* approach by prognosis approach. To speed up the development programmes in rural areas we need to involve Divisional Commissioners in the implementation and monitoring of rural development programmes on Haryana pattern. In Haryana they have been nominated as area officers to act as true 'ombudsman' for rural development programmes. This will certainly bring efficiency in the system and the level of corruption and crime will be brought down.

Removal of CC in India may be a utopian idea but we can certainly reduce the number of crimes and cases of corruption by taking some policy decisions. There should be time framework for the investigating agencies such as CID, CBI to submit their reports within 30 days of the happening of the crime. The long delays in submitting the reports by these agencies gives the impression that justice delayed is justice denied.

To remove CC in rural development programmes, we need to practice the 'zero tolerance against corruption'. Of course, there is need for protection for all those who accept and adopt zero tolerance against corruption as a challenge.

To remove poverty in rural India we have to improve the law and order situation. We need to integrate poverty issue in all development programmes. By removing corruption, in anti-poverty programmes it is firmly believed that we can increase annual growth rate of Gross Domestic Product by, at least, one percent otherwise it will take a long time to make India poverty and corruption free.

It is firmly believed by the author that for every ill of Indian Economy including rural sector there are Vedic pills and *Bhagwad Gita* is the panacea. It is not only a sacrosecular text for the entire humanity but a great epic of welfare economics. Its emphasis on humanistic values and on an optimistic future can certainly remove crime and corruption of both demand and supply side. It is essential for us, and particularly for the media persons to accept and adopt the implications of *Bhagwad Gita* which will certainly save India from the humiliation of being listed among the most corrupt nations in the world.

To bridge gap between rural development policy formation and its implementation, there is a strong case for providing opportunities for interaction between rural development reporters and the policy makers at all levels.

REFERENCES

Devasahayam, M.G. : Combating Supply side Corruption Effectiveness of C2 Principles, *The Tribune,* June 2000.

Goel, M.M.: Economics of Crime and Corruption in Indian Rural Development, IEA Conference (83rd) Volume of the Millennium 2000.

Sharma S.L.: Anatomy of Corruption, *The Tribune,* March 26, 2000.

Sinha, Ajit Kumar: Organised Crime and Political Economy of Development—The Indian Panorama, *The Indian Economic Journal,* Vol. 47 No. 3, Jan-March 1998-2000.

Swami Prabhupada: *Bhagwad Gita—As it is the Bhaktivedanta,* Book Trust International, Mumbai, 1972.

9

RURAL DEVELOPMENT AND MEDIA STRATEGY

R.S. DALAL

Eversince the beginning of economic planning, rural development has received an overriding priority. That is as it should be, because it was Mahatma Gandhi who said : Village development is the key to India's development. Rapid expansion of urban population notwithstanding a massive 629 million people (74.3 per cent of total population) constitute the rural population. Since the development of rural areas in terms of infrastructure, education and health care facilities had remained severely neglected for a number of years, it was, therefore, logical that planning should address the needs of rural areas urgently.

The Planning Commission defines Rural Development as : Rural development implies both the economic development of people as well as greater social transformation. Increased participation of the people in the rural development process, decentralisation of planning, better enforcement of land reforms and greater access to credit with better prospects for economic development. Improvement in health, education, drinking water, energy supply, sanitation and housing coupled with attitudinal changes also facilitates their social development.

Inspite of massive investments in the rural development and poverty alleviation programmes the benefits have not percolated down to the poor and the intended beneficiaries. Several factors have been responsible for such a situation : the existing power structure of village institution such as panchayats and cooperative societies which are captured by the rich and the politically influential people: centralised planning process emanating from the union Government and lack of awareness about the development programmes and projects available. It is now being increasingly realised that although we have a functioning government in our country, people have hardly any role in shaping their destinies at various levels which has severely affected the quality of governance in the country. The planning is mostly Delhi-centric; and the planning process concentrated in the offices of the Central Government and the Planning Commission. There have not been many people sponsored and village sponsored schemes.

There has been repeated criticism of the whole concept of development and the way the task of planned development was initiated and implemented. There has been greater realization that the economic betterment of the poor sections cannot be achieved without social transformation involving structural changes, educational development, growth in awareness, and change in outlook, motivation and attitudes. Social change can be achieved through greater participation of the poor by electing them to the grassroot level institutions. The Seventh Five Year Plan (1985-90) document says : Improvement of literacy and education, both through formal and non-formal means, and the imaginative use of the mass media for communicating useful information and knowledge as well as for changing the outlook of the people by instilling in them the egalitarian spirit, the urge for and confidence in achieving self betterment through cooperative endeavour, are essential for setting up the process of socio-economic transformation. It is now being frequently admitted that due to deficiencies noticed in the implementation of plan projects, illiteracy and lack of awareness on the part of beneficiaries, and chain of intermediaries, on the other hand, only a small portion of the intended outlay reaches the actual recipients.

Another serious drawback with our planning efforts is the centralised planning and approach to development.

The history of country's development planning shows that all measures to tackle poverty, generate employment and promote a more equitable socio-economic order through different programmes like Integrated Rural Development Programme (IRDP), Jawahar Rozgar Yojna (JRY), Drought Prone Areas Programme (DPAP), Small Farmers Development Agency (SFDA) have emanated from the centre. Several of the State Governments have not been very enthusiastic about these programmes.

One of our former Prime Ministers had gone on record saying that out of every rupee that the Centre spends on each of these schemes, only 20 paise reaches the targeted beneficiary. P. Sainath, the well known journalist who has made significant contribution to our understanding of rural poverty and whose book, *Everybody Loves a Good Drought, Stories from India's Poorest Districts,* gives a graphic account of rampant corruption prevailing at the grassroot level of development bureaucracy. He refers to one such instance, which is better if reproduced in his own words :

> A corrupt Block Development Officer (BDO) came. And what he said you cannot hear that even in a Bollywood film. He was asking for bribes from a few young people. He takes 25 per cent. If the work to be done in your village costs Rs. 10,000, then he should be given Rs. 2,500. This is the rate, it has to be given. He went to one village, Eshak village, a communist village. There was a young boy. He became emotional, it was the question of his pride, self-respect. Next day they came to the BDO's office and called him out. He had demanded 25 per cent, isn't it? Twentyfive young men came there and beat him 25 times with their *chappals.* Then the BDO filed a case of dacoity, brigandry, murder, etc., against these boys. When the case was in the process, I was there. The BDO was telling them, "I am willing to drop the cases, I bear you no grudge", he is a businessman. He was telling the leader of the group, "*are yarr, sir ko mara, dil ko mara, izzat ko mara arre hai pet me math maro*, give me my 25 per cent, I will

do your work and withdraw my case against you, I have got my transfer already." These kinds of negotiations were going on in the court right in front of everybody.

Media Strategy

It is only to curb the rampant corruption in rural development works that the campaign for Right to Information has been gathering strength in several States in the country. The movement in Rajasthan essentially aimed at ensuring accountability in development projects. The campaign was basically to obtain photocopies of bills, receipts, muster rolls and other documents concerning project accounts. The campaign got its inspiration from several *Jan sunwayis* (open public hearings) organised by the Mazdoor, Kisan Shakti Sangathan (MJSS) where hundreds of the poorest from far off villages came to speak, listen and share their experiences. Since the bureaucracy found such a movement challenging its authority, a stalemate ensured in getting any access to information legislation through.

The Indian press, by far the freest press in South Asia, pluralistic, multi-lingual, continues to be largely urban-oriented. More so the metropolitan press; and the newspapers coming out from the national capital are Delhi-centric. The press in English language is elitist geared to the commercial culture, obsessed with garnering the maximum share of advertising revenue. Issues concerning rural development are not given adequate coverage. In a study concerning content analysis of coverage of agricultural and rural development issues in four newspapers in English language, the researcher A.K. Singh concluded that small coverage given to these issues was due to the fact that these newspapers do not have substantial circulation in the rural areas and the professional interests of the newspapers are not served in any way by giving such news. The content analysis which included four newspapers—*The Hindu*, *Times of India*, *Hindustan Times* and the *Indian Express* for forty two days between January-June 1996 found that most of the contents of agricultural and rural development reporting were related to economic aspects rather than the ones relating to agricultural research and problems of agriculture. *The Hindu* was the only newspaper which regularly gave weekly page on various aspects of agriculture including the latest information in the field of research.

Reporting agricultural and rural issues is constrained by several factors : According to popular perceptions, rural development reporting is not considered glamorous or prestigious enough; in the reporter's scale of prestige, rural reporting occupies a low rung. Every young reporter dreams of covering politics, defence or foreign policy, rather than specialising in rural agricultural development reporting. Rural sector is so diffused and variegated including agricultural policies and operations, cooperatives, changing village milieu that it cannot be packaged into a neat, well defined slot. These and other constraints have relegated rural reporting to a back slot in an otherwise expanding media landscape in the country.

However, notwithstanding the above constraints there have been some outstanding examples of reporting rural development by leading newspapers in Kerala, specially *Malayala Manorama*, *Mathrubhoomi*, *Kerala Kaumudi* and *Desabhimani*. These newspapers have weekly farm feature pages which include articles, news stories, success stories of farmers, etc. with pictures. Some of these newspapers have taken to organising *kisan melas* and farmers' meets-functions which are generally performed by agricultural universities and research institutes. These farmers meets afford a valuable opportunity to farmers and farm experts to exchange information and views on various aspects of agriculture and associated areas. *Malayala Manorama* honours the best farmer of Kerala once in two years by awarding the title *Karshaka Sri*, a citation and Rs. 1 lakh. The panel of judges for the selection is led by two of world's most outstanding farm experts, Dr. M.S. Swaminathan and R.S.V. Kurien, both World Food Prize winners. The contribution made by the Malayalam press to agricultural development has been highlighted in an article by R. Hali in a special issue of *Kurukshetra* devoted to Media and Rural India. Hali concludes his article by saying : The Malayalam dailies have created a golden chapter in the history of creative development journalism by introducing the weekly farm feature page and running it for the last twenty years. Now every year, nearly 100 million pages are made available for farm news by the Malayalam dailies. They have really set a creative replicable model to the nation and to the developing countries.

Radio—The Tool for Rural Development

As a tool for development communication, reaching out to the people with relevant messages and usable information, and to encourage people's participation in the 'Open Forum' which it eventually provides; Community Radio is the ideal medium. Whereas in Sri Lanka Mahaweli Community radio network with 12 stations operating in remote rural areas have been the two successful examples in organising and operating community radio in India. The initiative to conceptualise, and promote community radio was taken by the *Voices* in 1996. As a communication resource and advocacy group, *Voices*—a Bangalore-based media NGO—has been spearheading a movement to examine issues relating to democratisation of media, the right to communicate and access to information and communication technologies particularly by the economically and socially deprived. The *Voices* plans to take up a one year pilot project which has been on air from Chitradurga FM Local Radio Station to gain experience and expertise, before actually setting up a community radio station.

It is interesting to note that several recent studies undertaken on media-related issues, clearly prove that, contrary to popular impression about marginalisation of radio, it continues to serve the village community effectively through its farm broadcasts. From the number of radio sets available and in use by the farmers in rural areas and the frequency and variety of programmes related to agriculture and rural development, including programmes like Farm Radio School, it is apparent that radio still enjoys primary importance in disseminating message of rural development. The policy makers and planners, in both the sectors—development as well as information and communication—need to re-order their priorities and densify, radio broadcasting—in terms of number of radio stations, availability of cheap radio sets and larger budgetary allocation for staff recruitment and upgradation of their knowledge and skills. The continued step motherly treatment meted out to radio broadcasting signifies a particular mind set of policy planners which is conditioned more by glamour and hightech hype rather than the hard realities of human condition of the rural poor and the marginalised sections of the Indian society.

That the Indian television has become primarily a medium for family entertainment and development programmes do not enjoy a large viewership has also been highlighted by a Doordarshan study. The study conducted by the Audience Research Unit of Doordarshan during January-March 1993, covering 420 villages from 15 States, observed that though Doordarshan entertainment programmes have a large viewership in villages, the development oriented programmes do not enjoy the same popularity. Some of the other findings of the study are :

1. Regional programmes are assumed to serve a very large area. Yet the programmes of Bangalore Kendra may not be relevant to the people in the northern districts of Karnataka. This lack of local specificity and context has a bearing on the viewership. The Doordarshan development programmes have, therefore, not been as effective as they should have been.
2. A total viewership of any programme is dependent not only on the rating, but also on the number of persons viewing from a set. A common observation is that in villages, domestic sets often become

community sets, attracting people from other households.

This study also collected information about the average number of persons watching a particular programme from one set, whereas nine viewers watched film-based programmes, only two opted for the programmes on agriculture.

Demystifying Media Profession

Knowledge, understanding and expertise in communication practice and profession should not be the exclusive prerogative of the media professionals. This need to be extended through a basic training course to all experts and workers at various levels working in the areas of rural development, health, sanitation and other nation-building activities. A basic appreciation of the elements of communication needs to be imparted through appropriate short-term courses. Media specialists, sociologists and development planners should work out inter-disciplinary mechanism for identifying the audience requirement, establishing proper feedback systems and extend guidance in the evaluation of effectiveness of communication programmes.

Extension Agency Reinforcement

Radio and TV broadcasting, essentially a part of mass media communication process, share the characteristics and limitations of such a system. In such a system amount of feedback readily available is low, the message flow tends to be one-way and can be used to increase knowledge. Interpersonal medium, on the other hand, tends to be two-way, the amount of feedback readily available is high and is best used in situations calling for attitude formation and change.

Interpersonal medium of communication, which in the context of rural development would include extension workers in the agriculture and community development departments of the State Governments, personnel of agricultural agencies like MFALA and agro-industries centres and extension set-up of agricultural universities and research institutes, would provide necessary reinforcement and supplement media programmes. Coordination between extension agencies and rural broadcasting will make these programmes more purposive and meaningful. These agencies, can in fact, help disseminate information about media programmes including subjects for discussion through numerous magazines, leaflets, folders they bring out regularly and on special occasions like farmers' fairs and field days, as a part of their extension activities. Programme producers and planners need to be suitably involved in modifying programmes to suit the requirement of the target audience.

A noteworthy initiative in crystallising interest in the conditions of the rural poor and marginalised sections of society from all over the country has recently been taken by the Press Institute of India by launching the monthly tabloid in English and Hindi—*Grassroots*. Expressing the rationale of taking up the initiative, the doyen of the Indian journalists and the Director, Press Institute of India Ajit Bhattacharjea says : The overall picture projected by the national press is ugly. It portrays an acquisitive, conflict ridden, middle class society, eager to achieve western standards of affluence, but unconcerned with the condition of human infrastructure at its base. And so we find nothing in the papers about panchayats, and empowerment, agriculture and the rual economy, literacy, unemployment, social tension. Yet without such coverage, the press fails its democratic function of monitoring the condition of society as a whole. It cannot claim the status of the Fourth Estate.

The *grassroots* brings to its readers the news stories from Andhra villages in search of drinking water, right to information compaign in Rajasthan and the success stories of NGOs. The August issue highlights the exploitation of Orissa tribals for bauxite (the adverse impact on the local population of alumina and bauxite mining projects located on tribal land in the Rayagada) and the November issue announces award for best feature to Richard Mahapatra on villagers protecting forests in Orissa.

REFERENCES

Doordarshan (1993). Television and its Impact on Rural Areas—A Doordarshan Study. In : (eds.) Dua, M.R. and Gupta, V.S., *Media and Development*. Har-Anand Publications, New Delhi.

Gupta, V.S. (1989). Case Study of Indian Rural Television. The Krishi Darshan Programme, *Media Asia* **16**(4): 215-218.

Gupta, V.S. and Rajeshwar Dyal (eds.) (1995). *Rural Press—Problems and Prospects*. Concept Publishing Company, New Delhi.

Grassroots (1999). Reporting the human condition (1-7) Press Institute of India, New Delhi.

Sainath, P. (1998). Fact and Fiction in *Exploring the Heartland*, An Agenda for the Media, Press Institute of India, New Delhi.

Sainath P. (1996). *Everybody Loves a Good Drought, Stories from India's Poorest Districts*. Penguin Books. India, New Delhi.

Voices (1997). Consultation on Media Policy and Community Radio. Workshop Report, Bangalore.

10

LANGUAGE PRESS AND NATIONAL DEVELOPMENT

VIR BALA AGGARWAL

The growth of the language press in India during the closing decades of the twentieth century truly reflects the diversity and plurality of rich linguistic and cultural heritage of the century. The Indian Constitution recognises 19 official languages which is an expression of India's cultural richness and linguistic diversity. In the modern mass media, as well as in traditional communication, the use of variety of languages is an advantage, bringing a large segment of user population on to equal terms of comprehension with other linguistic groups.

Interestingly, the Report of the International Commission for the Study of Communication Problems, *Many Voices One World,* lists 16 languages which are spoken by more than 50 million people; out of which there are 6 languages in which newspapers are published in India. These languages are—Hindi, Bengali, Urdu, Telugu and Tamil.

Small newspapers coming out from district centres and having grassroot contacts, mostly in Hindi and Indian languages, constitute another important segments of the Indian Press. These papers articulate the aspiration-demands, difficulties and problems of their readers and have been able to establish strong emotional affinity with them.

The Indian language press has played a historic and memorable role not only in the growth and development of journalism in the country, but also in the struggle for freedom movement. In the early nineteenth century it also concerned itself with the social reforms and religious issues of the period. With the emergence of Mahatma Gandhi on the Indian political scene and his non-cooperation movement, language papers extended the moral strength to the movement.

In his book, *Journalism in India,* Rangaswami Parthasarathy recapitulates the glorious contribution of the language press as under :

> Ill-equipped and with poor resources they managed to survive the onslaught and persecution of the alien rulers for over three decades and many of them fell on the wayside after writing a glorious chapter in the history of the freedom struggle during their brief existence. Many were the acts of courage and patriotism and sacrifice by the men who conducted these papers. They were dedicated to a cause and nothing could stop them from completing their mission. They endured privation and penury and even suffered imprisonment and when not there to enjoy the fruits of a hard-won battle but their spirits must have hovered over the battlements where they fought and sacrificed their lives to shed tears of joy. The contribution of Hindi and Urdu journalism to the struggle for freedom and the political awakening of the masses is immense.

The establishment of the Indian National Congress in 1885 further strengthened the nationalist aspirations of the Indian people. Most prominent members of the Congress were eminent towering personalities as Dadabhai Naoroji, Ranade, Narendranath Sen, etc. The Indian language press was particularly strong in expressing its views against the government.

A number of India's great men, social reformers, leaders and crusaders in the struggle of freedom movement used Press for furthering their philosophy and the causes they espoused. Some of these—Aurobindo Ghosh, Annie Besant, Lajpat Rai, Surendra Nath Banerji, Lokmanya Tilak and Mahatma Gandhi—were eminent journalists in their own right. Tilak carried on struggle for national liberation through journalism. He used the Marathi weekly *Kesari* and the English weekly *Maratha* for writing on social, political and economic subjects for the education and enlightenment of the people. Tilak used journalism for "popular education and public agitation".

The language press has evolved its own pattern responding to the demands and requirements of its readers. It accords proper importance to local and regional news as compared to national and international news which is generally received through news agencies. The events, problems and regional specific news, which are generally not treated adequately by the metropolitan press are of special interest to the language press. The language newspapers closer as they are to the local communities reflect the cultural and literary traditions of the people they serve.

A unique feature of the language press in the East and North-East Bengali, Assamese and Oriya is the vibrant practice of bringing special numbers and literacy supplements on festive occasions of Rangoli Bihu and Durga Puja. These special issues are brought out in large numbers and contain short stories, poems, creative writings and novels in full or serialised. Buying a Puja number is a part of the traditional festival shopping. Thus, these newspapers meet the higher literary and cultural aesthetics of the people and help mould their tastes. Elaborating the contribution of the language press in Orissa, Bhatt says :

> In Orissa's march ahead and particularly its cultural revival journalism has played no mean part. The press took literature to the people instead of allowing it to remain the preserve of the elite. The result is there for all to see the recognition that Oriya literature has earned by way of the Jananapeeth awards for its poetry and other forms of literature. The *Prajatantra* group brings out an English weekly, the *Eastern Times*, its *Jhankar* monthly has a high standing in Orissa for the quality of its literary material and for the awards it gives to writers which are prized.

The language press in the South has been particularly vibrant. Several newspapers, *Eenadu* in Andhra Pradesh and *Malayala Manorama* in Kerala have established a new genre of journalism in different ways.

The Telugu daily *Eenadu* launched in 1974, first from Visakhapatnam and a year later from Hyderabad has district editions from almost Andhra districts, with circulation crossing 4 lakhs. The success of *Eenadu* is attributed primarily to the rising public demand for information, Ramoji Rao played crucial role in the victory of N.T. Rama Rao and the *Telugu Desam Party* in 1983. The newspaper has diversified its activities by launching its own regional TV channel and supports an English daily *Newstimes* from Hyderabad.

Because of the highest rate of literacy in the country, the people of Kerala enjoy a high degree of awareness and can therefore claim a large slice of language press. The country's highest circulated daily paper, the *Malayala Manorama*, enjoys a high level of prestige in terms of editorial quality, introduction of latest printing technology and taking initiative in promoting agricultural and rural development in the State. A multi-edition newspaper it has been the highest circulated daily in the country for several years.

Several other Indian language papers have also rendered valuable service in shaping different aspects of economic development, social awareness and cultural rejuvenation. This chapter has attempted a short overview of the progress of the Indian Language Press in the country about which Mark Tully in his book from *Raj to Rajiv* in 1989 had said : The Indian press, on the one hand must be most free and lively in the Third World. It does act as a watching on the government which is essential if democracy is to survive in India. There has been an explosion of papers and magazines in both English and Indian languages over the last fifteen years and journalism has become much more vigorous.

Language press constitutes one of the most important

media for reaching out to the hundreds of millions of people in all parts of the country. As an important link between planners, bureaucracy and the people at the grassroot level, language press is a viable mean for the promotion of literacy, social awareness and development.

However, it may be noted with concern that in their struggle for existence, the language newspapers sometimes do not adhere to the ethics of journalism i.e. truthfulness and responsibility, objectivity and fair play. Development or literacy related news is far from their mind. Their main objective is to increase sales. The contents and presentation of such papers have a focus on the entertainment, negative news, mainly pertaining to violence, theft, political instability, scams, etc. No doubt these are required for wider dissemination. But the coverage of news of positive side of human life and society should also be there.

Problems Encountered by Language Press

The language press is not only ignored but also scorned by the elite as well as the government. It is felt that the language press is to face more years of persistent struggle ahead before it is recognised as a significant segment of the Indian press along with English/National dailies. Various other problems which come in the way of reporting in case of language press are : financial problems, availability of information and authenticity thereof, infrastructural facilities, risks and threats involved keeping in view the castes, communities and groupism factors. The main challenge before the language reporting in language press is to sensitize the elite readership towards developmental issues affecting the Indian masses, the vast majority of which is inhabiting the rural areas. The nexus of illiteracy, poverty, poor health can be broken by the language press by focusing on the developing schemes, in vogue, and promoting the role of voluntary organisations to break the bureaucratic bottlenecks in the welfare and development schemes. It has been observed that the personnel working in the language press lack adequate training required to handle their multifaceted responsibilities. It may be suggested that an appreciation course in language problems preferably by a language institute or an agricultural university would go a long way in redressing this deficiency.

Language press is a promising medium for disseminating information and knowledge about nutrition, health and hygiene, improved farm practices, family planning measures and development plans to those sections of society where the information is needed most. Hence it becomes all the more important to help in the promotion and sustenance of language press through various measures.

What is needed is to make language press relevant to the Indian situation. It has to encompass in itself the cultural ethos of the Indian life in all its aspects mainly the rural poor and unrepresented people in the press. Its subjects would include profile of an artisan, success story of a farmer, neoliterate women, literacy worker or even the failure stories for reflections, problems faced in marketing of agricultural produce, social superstitions and taboos inhibiting the economic growth and productivity. Such kind of language press shall not only mirror the true life in the Indian people, but shall also provide a different perspective and frame of reference for the planners and policy makers to improve the quality of life of people through literacy and development. The language press is required to assume the role of the information centre about various schemes, plants, projects, weather forecast reports and facilities available like credit, seed, fertilizer besides new development projects e.g. construction of a new road or a bridge in the far flung areas.

Promoting the Language Press for Literacy and Development

Some of the important policy and remedial measures which may help in the promotion and sustenance of language press are :

1. Local papers should be allowed to be printed at the Government Press on subsidised rates.
2. Provision of free bus and railway passes for the editors of language papers should be there, at par with big newspapers.
3. Journalists of language newspapers should be provided free insurance and legal protection. There should also be proper police protection for them.
4. Paper quota for these papers should be provided on control rates by the government.
5. Facilities for loans under various schemes of the government should also be there as for other cottage industries.
6. The advertisements of various government departments, banks, public sector undertakings should be routed through the D.P.R.O. who should then distribute it proportionately to the local press.
7. Language/Local papers should not be discouraged by the local administration but due importance must be given to their coverage. They should rather be interacted with, encouraged and given positive direction by organising workshops/camps from time to time.
8. It should be the endeavour of the language press to associate itself with various organisations and departments working in the Indian society, especially they must participate in their functions.
9. The language press is required to have closer association and links with the local bodies such as village panchayats and also with the opinion makers in the villages to promote the development in indigenous situation.
10. Indian Languages Press Commission should be appointed to go into whole gamut of the working of language press.
11 Language press should aim at the community service and development. It should be the mirror of the true life of human society. It should be true

source of feed-back to the government and policy makers. But at the same time, while having such expectations from the language press, the latter should also expect co-operation from the government and the public at large.

11

COVERAGE OF HEALTH AND NUTRITION ISSUES IN NATIONAL DAILIES

SAROJ DAHIYA

Mass media are an integral part of national development especially in conveying information (Agarwal, 1993).

The print media is one of the oldest means of communication still being used in all the stages of life on a large scale and has brought revolution as well as modernisation in society (Schramm, 1964).

A newspaper is such an answer book which has got lakhs of examiners. It works as the eyes and the ears of the readers. Newspapers serve people in three ways—they inform, guide and entertain. If used properly these can also be employed effectively and have the ability of reaching a large number of people simultaneously and quickly, these are also a low cost medium. Press which is powerful medium of public opinion and social change is supposed to reflect the activity of society especially those related to education, gender and health. Some newspapers have started allotting certain space to discuss health problems in addition to the coverage of news on them.

Many newspapers have started health column which includes significant articles and features relevant to health and nutrition in making them aware about health and nutrition such as "Health Tribune" in *The Tribune*. Wednesday Editions in *The Tribune* usually have a column for coverage of health and nutrition in which news related to some disease and its prevention, health and physical fitness, food and beauty/health are published.

Health education is an essential tool of community health. Health education is required to play a much more expanded and critical role in the developing countries where nutritional deficiencies, communicable diseases still are major causes of morbidities and mortalities (UNICEF, 1986).

On an average space allotted to health and nutrition issues varies from one to nearly two per cent in most of the newspapers. A critical insight into the review revealed that in India most of the print media studies have been in the area of content analysis of agriculture information. Very little attempts have been made to know qualitative as well as quantitative coverage of health and nutrition issues in newspapers.

Keeping in view the above perspectives, the present study was undertaken to analyse in the quantitative term, the nature, extent and present trends of health and nutrition issues reported by selected National Dailies.

METHODOLOGY

Selection of Newspapers

According to reports of Audit Bureau of Circulation, 1977, *The Indian Express* since 1955 (1997), no Indian language paper could be considered as national newspaper. The criteria for classifying a newspaper as national newspaper is given below :

(i) All India average circulation per day and for particular year.

(ii) How diverse and widespread the readership is i.e. in how many States and Union Territories the newspaper is circulated.

All the selected papers have wide all-India circulation. *The Times of India* is published from six places and *The Hindustan Times* from two places.

Sample Selection

For ensuring fairly representative analysis the five selected

English newspapers viz. *The Hindustan Times*, *The Indian Express*, *The Hindu* and *The Times of India* all published from New Delhi and *The Tribune* from Chandigarh for the period 1-30 June, 1999 constituted the universe of study. The Food and Nutrition issues published in all the selected newspapers for the above mentioned period comprised the sample of study.

Selection of Health and Nutrition Issues

Food and nutrition issues are the concerns which people want to know daily for maintaining good health. These concerns including physical fitness and exercise, role of food in health and disease, recipes are taken up by the media time to time. Purposive selection of health and nutrition issues was made.

All editorials, articles, features, news, advertisements, middle, letters to the editor and photographs with or without clear head lines in which health and nutrition was focussed or any other item which was directly related to foods and nutrition were included in the content.

Categorization of Selected Issues

The sample coverage given to food and nutrition was distributed over various categories of issues for determining the relative significance attached to the issues. The categories evolved were : Role of food in health and diseases, Cookery/recipes with photographs, Present food trends, Recent health and nutrition care and techniques, Health/ nutrition programmes, Advances in food science and technology, Foods in advertisements, Epidemiology and management of diseases, Nutritional quality of conventional and non-conventional foods, Food quality, control and malpractices, and Nutrition during life cycle .

Analysis and Interpretation of Content

All the published information on selected issues was analysed quantitatively as well as qualitatively.

Quantitative Analysis

Quantitative analysis indicates the contents to which the health and nutrition issues are being covered by the papers. The present study includes :

(i) Total space allotted to health and nutrition issues in relation to total space of the newspaper.

(ii) Space covered by different categories of health and nutrition issues.

(iii) Space covered by sub-categories of health and nutrition issues.

Qualitative Analysis

Qualitatively the content was analysed in terms of source of coverage, format of coverage, context of coverage and placement of coverage regarding health and nutrition issues.

Analysis and Interpretation of Content

Statistical tools used for analysis of data were as follows :

Total used measures	*Purpose*
Column centimetre	Space accorded to categories and sub-categories of health and nutrition issues were measured column-wise in centimetres using a scale.
Percentage and rank	Space covered by different health and nutrition issues, space of information used, format of coverage, context of coverage and placement of coverage.

RESULTS AND DISCUSSIONS

General Information about Selected National Dailies

Results revealed that out of five English Dailies, *The Times of India* had the maximum average number of pages (36) followed by *The Hindustan Times* (30), *The Hindu* (24) and *The Indian Express* (23). *The Tribune* had only 20 pages. Regarding total average printed area, again *The Times of India* was found to be at the top having average printed area (16822.8 col. cms) followed by *The Hindustan Times* (12772.6 col. cms), and *The Hindu* (9984.2 col. cms). *The Indian Express* and *The Tribune* were found to have 8211.5 col. cms and 9875.8 col. cms average printed area, respectively.

Analysis of number of subscribers of all the selected dailies (as on 15.11.99) in Hissar city revealed that maximum readership was in favour of *The Hindustan Times* (2300) followed by *The Times of India* (1950), and The Tribune (1600) whereas only 130 and 140 subscribers were credited to *Thc Indian Express* and *The Hindu*, respectively. Thus, it can be inferred from the data that in the present study, *The Hindustan Times* was found to be the most popular paper and had maximum number of subscribers in Hissar city.

Total Space devoted to Health and Nutrition Issues

Data have been presented in Table 11.1 which gives the total number of items related to health and nutrition issues in relation to total average printed area of the papers. Analysis showed that *The Indian Express* was leading as far as the number of items (35) was concerned. *The Times of India* was found to have least number i.e. 15 items only. As regards proportion of total space (col. cms) devoted to health and nutrition issues in all the dailies, it was found that maximum space was covered in *The Hindu* (202 col. cms). *The Times of India* and *The Indian Express* had total space devoted to health and nutrition as 114.0 col. cms and 192 col. cms, respectively.

It is clear from the Table 11.1 that percentage space coverage by health and nutrition issues accounted maximum (2.33%) in *The Indian Express* and the minimum (0.67%) in *The Times of India*.

TABLE 11.1 : Total Space and Number of Items devoted to Health and Nutrition Issues

Sr. No.	Main areas of information	National dailies (English)				
		The Times of India	*The Hindustan Times*	*The Indian Express*	*The Hindu*	*The Tribune*
1.	Total average printed area of the papers (col. cms.)	16876.8	12776.5	8211.0	9984.0	9248.0
2.	Total number of items present	2210	1392	1500	1085	900
3.	Total number of items related to health and nutrition issues	15	21	35	22	23
4.	Total space covered by health and nutrition issues (col. cms.)	114	198	192	202	199
5.	Percentage space covered by health and nutrition issues	0.57	1.54	2.33	2.02	2.15

The results clearly showed that insufficient coverage was devoted to health and nutrition issues by all the dailies. This indicates the least importance given to health and nutrition issues by the press. This finding about the proportion of total space devoted to health issues is not very different from one reported by Kubde and Sinha (1987) who concluded that health and agriculture news are not

TABLE 11.2 : Distribution of Health and Nutrition related Items in Five National Dailies according to Content Categories

Sr. No.	*Categories of health and nutrition issues*	*HT*	*TOI*	*IE*	*TH*	*The Tribune*
1.	Role of food in health and diseases	—	3 (20.00)	4 (11.42)	1 (4.55)	—
2.	Cookery/recipes with photographs	2 (9.52)	4 (26.66)	7 (20.00)	2 (9.09)	7 (30.43)
3.	Present food trends	1 (4.76)	—	—	—	—
4.	Recent health and nutrition care and techniques	3 (14.28)	5 (33.33)	6 (17.14)	3 (13.63)	4 (17.39)
5.	Health/nutrition programmes	2 (9.52)	1 (6.66)	2 (5.71)	3 (13.63)	—
6	Advances in food science and technology	4 (19.04)	2 (13.33)	3 (8.57)	6 (27.26)	2 (8.69)
7.	Food in advertisements	1 (4.76)	—	3 (8.57)	1 (4.54)	1 (4.34)
8.	Epidemiology and management of diseases	2 (9.52)	—	5 (14.28)	4 (18.18)	5 (21.73)
9.	Nutritional quality of foods	5 (23.80)	—	3 (8.57)	—	3 (13.04)
10.	Food quality, control and malpractices	1 (4.76)	—	1 (2.85)	2 (9.09)	—
11.	Nutrition during life cycle	—	—	1 (2.85)	—	1 (4.34)
	Total No. of items	21	15	35	22	23

Note : Figures in parentheses denote percentages.
HT – *Hindustan Times*
TOI – *Times of India*
IE – *Indian Express*
TH – *The Hindu*
TTR – *The Tribune*

given due priority as against the crime and political news in seven region of Vidarbha (Nagpur).

Distribution of Different Categories of Health and Nutrition related Issues in Five National Dailies

Table 11.2 shows the relative number of different health and nutrition issues published in the selected dailies.

A perusal of Table 11.2 reveals that maximum number (22 items) related to category cookery/recipes with photographs were published in all the five national dailies during the period of study. Whereas total of 21 items related to recent health and nutrition care and techniques were observed in all the papers followed by items related to epidemiology and management of different diseases. Percentage-wise analysis showed that in *The Hindustan Times*, the maximum percentage (23.80%) of news published were related to nutritional quality of conventional and unconventional foods followed by advances in food science and technology (19.04%) and cooking (9.05%). There was no news or role of food in health and disease and nutrition during life cycle and only one advertisement related to health and nutrition was found published in *The Hindustan Times*. In *The Times of India*, maximum (33.33%) coverage was of recent health/nutrition care followed by cookery (26.66%). Other aspects like nutrition during life cycle, food quality control, nutritional quality of foods received very low coverage. There was no advertisement related to this subject published in *The Times of India*. *The Indian Express* also covered mostly issues related to cookery and recent health/nutrition techniques. *The Indian Express* published almost all the news related to different categories. *The Hindu* covered mostly news related to advances in food science and technology (27.76%) followed by epidemiology and management of diseases and cookery (9.0%). Nutritional quality of foods and nutrition during life cycle were totally ignored in *The Hindu*.

As regards *The Tribune*, cookery occupied maximum number of space (30.43%) followed by news related to epidemiology of diseases and control measures (16 items) and advance in food science and technology (15 items). Analysis further showed that out of 116 items only one item was related to present food trends and 2 items were published related to nutrition during life cycle.

So it can be inferred from the Table 11.2 that the news related to cookery advances in food science and recent health nutrition techniques for disease control were published more as compared to other aspects i.e. nutrition during life cycle, nutritional quality of food, food quality control and role of food in health and disease which are very important issues to be known by the people. It is, therefore, the duty of the press council to get the journalists trained in the field of health and foods and nutrition and encourage them to write such articles in the papers.

Source of Information used for Reporting Health and Nutrition Issues

Table 11.3 reveals that most of the health and nutrition issues were by the newspaper's own correspondents (22.0%) and 19.04 per cent items each covered by *The Times of India* and *The Hindustan Times* respectively. Similarly around one-third i.e. 31.43 per cent items published in *The Indian Express* and *The Tribune* were by their correspondents themselves.

Maximum number of items were published by freelance journalists (40.00, 47.61, 40.00, 40.90 and 34.78%) in *The Times of India, The Hindustan Times, The Indian Express, The Hindu* and *The Tribune*, respectively. The items covered by news agencies (national as well as international) reflected relatively less efforts in all the dailies as compared to items filed by the dailies own correspondents, freelance journalists and manufacturing companies. Photographs were observed to be the least important source of information in the case of *The Times of India* and *The Indian Express*. Letters to the Editor were not found as a source of information in all the dailies except in *The Indian Express* where one letter related to health and

TABLE 11.3 : Sources of Information used for reporting Health and Nutrition Issues

Sr. No.	Sources of information used	National Dailies									
		The Times of India		*The Hindustan Times*		*The Indian Express*		*The Hindu*		*The Tribune*	
		No. of Items	*Rank*	*No. of Items*	*Rank*	*No. of Items*	*Rank*	*No. of Items*	*Rank*	*No. of Items*	*Rank*
1.	Newspapers own correspondents	3 (20.00)	II	4 (19.04)	II	11 (31.43)	II	3 (13.63)	II	7 (30.43)	II
2.	National wire service	2 (13.33)	III	2 (9.52)	IV	2 (5.71)	IV	2 (9.09)	III	2 (8.70)	III
3.	International wire service	1 (6.66)	V	2 (9.52)		3 (8.57)	III	2 (9.09)	III	2 (8.70)	III
4.	Freelance journalists	6 (40.00)	I	10 (47.61)	I	14 (40.00)	I	9 (40.90)	I	8 (34.78)	I
5.	Manufacturing company	1 (6.66)	V	1 (4.76)	III	–	–	3 (13.63)	II	2 (8.70)	III
6.	Letters to the editor	–		–		1 (2.85)	V	–	–	–	–
7.	Photographs	–		1 (4.76)		2 (5.71)	IV	1 (4.54)	IV	1 (4.35)	IV
8.	No source mentioned	2 (13.33)	IV	1 (4.76)		2 (5.71)	IV	2(9.09)	III	1 (4.35)	IV
9.	Total No. of items	15		21		35		22		23	

Note : Figures in parentheses denote percentages.

nutrition was published during the period of analysis. Rahul (1994) and Sangwan (1998) also reported that press correspondents of the newspapers were important source of information. This may be due to the fact that most of the items related to health and nutrition were found to be covered in supplements/additional pages of Sunday issues or one regular page once in a week and these were mostly written by freelance journalists.

Next important source of coverage was advertisement by manufacturing companies. The reason for wider coverage of items in the form of advertisements may be economic factor because advertisements make it possible and worthwhile to run the paper regularly. The findings are in tune with the findings of Sharma (1994), Sangwan (1998), Sindhu (1977) and Vijayaraghvan (1997).

Format of Coverage regarding Health and Nutrition Issues

Table 11.4 clearly shows that as far as news items are concerned, 66.66 per cent in *The Times of India*, 57.14 per cent in *The Hindustan Times*, 45.71 per cent in *The Indian Express* were published during the period of analysis. Whereas in *The Hindustan Times* and *The Tribune* 59.09 and 52.17 per cent news items were published respectively related to health and nutrition. As far as advertisements are concerned, *The Hindu* had maximum number of advertisements (9.09%) followed by *The Tribune* (8.69%) whereas *The Times of India* had no advertisement related to health and nutrition issues. As regards editorials, *The Indian Express* published one editorial (2.85%). *The Times of India* had no photograph related to health and nutrition issues.

It is clear from Table 11.4 the coverage of health and nutrition issues suffer from both inadequacy and distortion. The nutritional issues seem to be the least thing on the agenda of *The Indian Express*. The majority of the valuable space in all the selected dailies was taken up by politics, economics and other developmental news. There was no

TABLE 11.4 Format of Coverage regarding Health and Nutrition Issues

Sr. No.	*Format of coverage*	*TOI*	*HT*	*IE*	*TH*	*The Tribunal*
1.	Articles	3 (20.00)	4 (19.04)	5 (14.28)	3 (13.63)	5 (21.73)
2.	Features	2 (13.33)	3 (14.28)	7 (20.0)	3 (13.63)	3 (13.04)
3.	News	10 (66.66)	12 (57.14)	16 (45.71)	13 (59.09)	12 (52.17)
4.	Advertisements	–	1 (4.76)	3 (8.57)	2 (9.09)	2 (8.69)
5.	Editorials	–	–	1 (2.85)	–	–
6.	Letters to the editor	–	–	1 (2.85)	–	–
7.	Photographs	–	1 (4.76)	2 (5.71)	1 (4.54)	1 (4.34)
	Total No. of items	15	21	35	22	23

Note : The figures in brackets denote percentage.

cartoon published relating to health and nutrition issues in all the dailies. Regarding photographs, except for *The Times of India*, all the papers had photographs related to health and nutrition issues with maximum number in *The Indian Express*. This finding is in agreement with that of Prasad (1992) and Sangwan (1998) who reported that in selected five dailies there were no editorial, no cartoons during the period of study.

Context and Placement of Coverage Regarding Health and Nutrition Issues

Table 11.5 indicates the level of reporting of health and nutrition issues whether it was national, international, district or village level. Data showed that in all the dailies, maximum coverage related to health and nutrition issues was in the form of features, articles, news items, photographs and advertisements ranging from 57.14 per cent in *The Indian Express* followed by 39.13 per cent in

TABLE 11.5 : Context of Coverage regarding Health and Nutrition Issues

Sr. No.	*Context of coverage*	*HT*	*TOI*	*IE*	*TH*	*The Tribunal*
1.	International	6 (28.57)	2 (13.33)	4 (11.42)	7 (31.81)	1 (4.35)
2.	National	2 (9.52)	2 (13.33)	5 (14.28)	3 (13.63)	2 (8.70)
3.	State level	2 (9.52)	3 (20.00)	4 (11.42)	1 (4.54)	3 (13.05)
4.	District level	1 (4.76)	2 (13.33)	1 (5.71)	1 (4.54)	6 (26.10)
5.	Village level	0	0	1 (2.85)	0	2 (8.70)
6.	Others (photographs, features and articles)	10 (47.61)	6 (39.99)	20 (57.14)	10 (45.45)	9 (39.13)
	Total No. of items	21	15	35	22	23

Note : Figures in parentheses denote percentage.

The Tribune, 47.60 per cent in *The Hindustan Times* whereas it was the lowest in *The Times of India* (39.99%). International level reportage came next as 31.81 per cent in *The Hindu*, 28.57 per cent in *The Hindustan Times* whereas 4.35 per cent in *The Tribune*. About 9.52 per cent of the items in *The Hindu*, 13.33 per cent in *The Times of India* and 8.70 per cent in *The Tribune* were of national level. It is clear that little number of items (11) were related to different districts. *The Tribune* published maximum (26.10%) district level news followed by 13.33 per cent in *The Times of India* and very less news of district level was found in *The Hindu* and *The Hindustan Times*.

Further it was surprising to observe that the rural reportage got very small coverage, as compared to urban reporting with maximum (8.70%) in *The Tribune* only as compared to other dailies. The findings are in close agreement with those of Kudbe and Sinha (1987) who also found less news on rural health. Thus, it can be inferred from the data that health and nutrition coverage is mostly restricted to insignificant photographs. Problems and issues have not been discussed in depth at any level by any of the selected national dailies.

Regarding placement of coverage of health and nutrition issues, it was found that in *The Tribune*, health and nutrition issues were given on Health Tribune page and supplement (feature page) of Sunday issue. In *The Hindustan Times*, majority of health and nutrition issues were covered in supplement (feature page/national page or local city page) whereas in *The Times of India*, majority of the news items were found on supplements/local city pages.

Health and nutrition issues were not found on front page/career page or last page/classified advertisement page in all the papers. These findings are in agreement with those reported by Gupta, B.R. (1998).

Summary and Conclusions

Results revealed that as regards percentage space coverage, health and nutrition issues ranged from 0.67 to 2.33 in the selected dailies. There was great variation among the newspapers about the topics covered. With the highest space coverage in *The Indian Express* and the lowest in *The Times of India* and proportion of space devoted to health and nutrition items was less in all the papers.

In *The Hindustan Times* the maximum percentage and space (23.8 col. cms) of health and nutrition published were covered under nutritional quality of foods, in *The Times of India* under health/nutrition care and techniques (33.75 col. cms), in *The Hindu* advances in food science and technology (35.21 col. cms). *The Tribune* published mostly items related to cookery/recipes whereas *The Indian Express* covered almost all the areas except recent food trends.

The coverage of health and nutrition issues suffers from inadequacy and distortion. Issues like food quality control, and nutrition during life cycle were totally ignored in all the selected dailies. Issues like recent health/nutrition care and techniques occupied maximum space followed by cookery/recipes, advances in food science and technology, epidemiology and management of diseases and nutritional quality of foods in all the newspapers. The important issues i.e. role of food in health and disease, present food consumption and production trends and various health/

nutrition schemes introduced by government received meagre coverage in all the papers. Press correspondence of the papers and freelance journalists were important source of information about health and nutrition in all the papers. International coverage of these issues was found to be more in all the papers under analysis followed by national and regional except in *The Tribune*, which covered more regional news as compared to international and national. There were very few items on the front page in all the papers and in *The Tribune* and *The Indian Express* the items were published on regular days. Regarding format of coverage, it was found that mostly health and nutrition items were in the news form followed by articles and features with few advertisements and photographs in all the papers. Except in *The Indian Express*, no paper had published editorial and letter to the editor related to these issues. All the papers were found creating awareness completely about health and nutrition issues. Most of the health and nutrition items were published in the form of news items followed by articles and features.

It is thus recommended that it is the responsibility of the journalists to carry out advocacy campaigns on various issues which will faster the development process. It is suggested that the newspaper management should encourage training programme for the staff and journalists in the field of health and nutrition. NGOs should take initiative in disseminating news about such issues. Regular dissemination of research news by research institutions will go a long way in creating awareness on such issues.

Acknowledgement

The author wishes to express her deep acknowledgement to Prof. V.S. Gupta for his able guidance in carrying out this study.

NOTE

The study has carried out in partial fulfilment of the requirement of PG Diploma in Agriculture Journalism at CCS Haryana

Agricultural University, Hissar for 1999-2000 session. The study was adjudged as the best in the group.

REFERENCES

Agarwal, B.C. (1993). Development communication. A historical and contemporary perspective. *Interaction*, 2: 2.

Gupta, B.R. (1998). Development Journalism in India : A study of leading newspapers. Ph.D. thesis submitted to B.H.U., Varanasi.

Kubde, V.R. and R.R. Sinha (1987). Space distribution and categories of rural news coverage in Regional Dailies of Vidarbha. *Maharashtra Journal of Extension Education*, 6: 169-172.

Prasad, Nandini (1992). *A Pressing Matter : Women in Press.* Friedrich Ebert Stiftung, New Delhi.

Rahul (1994). A profile of local newspapers of Hissar. Project Report submitted to the Indian Institue of Mass Communication, New Delhi.

Sangwan, V. (1998). Women's issues in print media. A study of national dailies. M.Sc. Thesis, CCS HAU, Hissar.

Schramm, Wilbur (1964). *Mass Media and National Development. The Role of Information in Developing of Countries.* Stanford, California, Stanford University.

Sharma, N. (1996). Channels of health communication in rural India. *Interaction*, 2: 108.

Sindhu, D.K. (1997). Coverage of environment by print media. *Communicator*, 31(1): 20.

UNICEF (1986). *Micro Planning and Management Course in EPI.* Users manual for multipurpose workers Part II. UNICEF, Regional Office for South Central Asia, New Delhi, p. 5.

Vijayaraghvan, R. (1997). General reading behaviour of farm families. *Journal Extension Education*, 8(4): 1855.

12

MEDICAL JOURNALISM
Emergence of a New Genre

RAVI K. DHAR, SHEETAL THAPAR AND GEETU SHARMA

With the fragmentation of the media audiences into specialized target groups having their own specific agenda of uses and gratification from the media, the genre of journalism too has undergone subject specific fragmentation. The growth of health consciousness in the people of the developed world and disease-consciousness in the people of the developing world has spurred this Janus-faced process of fragmentation towards the evolution of medical/ health journalism.[1] No wonder, *Medline,* United States' National Library of Medicine's massive bibliographic database of medical research and publications, has abstracts of 9 million documents dating back to 1996, including articles in more than 3,900 medical related journals. This phenomenal growth is not restricted to the up-town research journals alone but extends to down-town popular magazines, newspapers and electronic media too. Health stories in the USA are now regularly carried on the front pages of newspapers and as daily segments on prime-time TV newscasts (Scott Eggener, 1998). Back home, the launching of the Indian edition of *British Medical Journal* by the Kasturba Medical College Trust in March 1985 ushered in a new era in medical journalism in India. In a short span of seventeen years, it has become the second largest circulated medical journal in India with a circulation as large as 25,000 and a respectable readership size of 75,000. Similarly, the publication of the Indian edition of *Pediatrics,* the official journal of the American Academy of Pediatrics (AAP), started in 1989, too has been a success story. Till date, it has become a popular journal among 12,000 pediatricians in India, as well as among the general practitioners. Besides, many national dailies and regional newspapers have a regular supplement/column on health and medicine. This shows the buoyancy of readers' interest in them. Magazines and e-zines have not been far behind, indicating the general groundswell of interest in medical journalism.

It is against the backdrop of this interest in medical journalism, that we have made a humble attempt at understanding the broad contours of the emergence of medical journalism as a new genre. To this end, the study attempts to achieve the following objectives:

(i) To try and understand what is implied by medical journalism,

(ii) To map the various forms that medical journalism has manifested in,

(iii) To look at medical journalism from the standpoint of the process model to understand the internal pyrotechnics of medical journalism, and

(iv) To evaluate medical journalism with the yardstick of ethics.

In keeping with the objectives of the study, the discussion has been divided into four sections. The first section deals with the meaning of medical journalism and its distinction with other related genres of journalism, the second with the forms of medical journalism, the third with medical journalism as seen through the process model and the fourth and the last section with the evaluation of medical journalism in its present incarnation.

Medical Journalism and Science and Health Journalism

Before we may attempt to understand the juggernaut of the emergence of medical journalism, we feel that we must not hesitate to answer basic questions such as: What is medical journalism? And how is it different from science and health journalism?

Science journalism, as its name indicates, dwells on everything that is related to science. As science is a very broad category of knowledge, it is inclusive of health and medical journalism. Coming to health journalism, we realize as its appellation indicates, that it deals with the larger gamut of health related issues, such as sanitation, pollution, nutrition and environmental issues etc. that the society needs to take care of if it wants its members to be free from avoidable maladies. Medical journalism, on the other hand, confines itself to focussing attention on the outbreak of diseases and their possible prevention and cure. There is an element of immediacy in medical journalism which health journalism lacks as it deals directly with diseases and their cure. It follows, therefore, that a biomedical writer[2] who writes on medical topics for a newspaper or a magazine may be called a medical journalist. Their stories could either be aimed at the general public or at the healthcare professionals themselves.

Medical journalism is a highly specialized genre of journalism which makes exacting subject specific demands from the medical journalists. The medical journalist must be precise and accurate in his/her coverage of medical news events in the writing of stories on medical topics, as these are most often acted upon by the general public, despite the general disclaimer advertised boldly in all medical publications.

As far as the site from which they write, they could be working in the news-rooms, corporations, hospitals, non-profit organizations, entertainment industries (programme on health as by Mukta Arts for both entertainment and information), schools, government agencies, health maintenance organizations and pharmaceutical firms.

Forms of Medical Journalism

Medical journalism is characterized by two extreme forms: on the one end are the high brow medical journals which cater to the specialized sections of medicos and on the other end are articles and reports carried by the mass-circulated magazines, newspapers, pamphlets, mailings, billboards, radio, television and the internet (Scott Eggener, 1998).

Due to the specialized character of the subject matter dealt with in medical journalism, the emergence of mass based medical journals/magazines depends a lot on the extent to which medics venture out of their medical cloisters to share medical information with the general reading public. Wherever it has happened, the result has been resounding as in the case of Dr. Rajeev Gupta's *Meditrack.*[3]

As technology does not act merely as a vehicle but also structures and modifies the media content according to its particular requirements, it would be rewarding to take a close look at the technology-specific forms of medical journalism, namely: print, electronic and online medical journalism.

A. Print

The print media is basically a text-based media with graphics and visuals coming in as reinforcements. Medical news stories and feature articles—both rely on the power of the word to capture the attention of the reader. But if the word is supplemented with pictures and illustrations, the effect is greater.

Newspapers in India have a limited number of columns or pages on health/medical issues. *The Tribune* publishes its health section every Wednesday. Besides, the magazines and journals published in India are as few as 60.

B. Electronic

The electronic media, as opposed to the print media, is a visual media and it thrives for its success on the 'spectacle'. The briefer the text, oral or written, the better it is for greater effect. So, the premium here is on precision. But, as it is time bound and commercialized, it may affect the quality of content. This is a serious disadvantage. Perhaps, that is why medical journalism in the electronic media relies on government support. However, as viewer interest in medical journalism continues to grow, TV channels are finding it lucrative enough to spare time slots for medical journalism. For instance, channels such as 'Discovery' are thorough and professionally slick in presenting medical stories in their telecasts.

C. Online

Online medical journalism is similar to electronic journalism except for one major departure. It is interactive and user-friendly, while the electronic is not. No wonder, practical computer exposure, with more advanced workshops and seminars is a valuable part of any science journalism programme. The e-health sites have a bounty of health and medical information available online. According to Alta Vista search engine, more than seventeen million web pages have the word 'Health' in them. In the USA, the main federal government's web page for medical data is the National Centre for Health Statistics (NCHS), part of the centres for disease control and prevention. It provides an easy access to statistics on major health care topics, on topics like incidence of common cold, average length of a hospital stay or how often people visit the doctor or dentist.

In India, many newspapers provide an extensive coverage of separate topics related to health and medicine on the web, for instance, *www.indiatimes.com* of *The Times of India* has columns like:

Health and Fitness
Alternative Medicine
Children's Health
Disease
Exercise and Fitness
Medical Equipment
Women's Health
Hospitals

Doctors
Yoga
International Sites
Child Birth
Weight Watches
Health Answers
World Health Organization

Similar are the sites of *tribuneindia.com* and *hindustantimes.com.*

In spite of the fact that online media provides excellent health resources, yet the standard of journalism on most health sites leaves much to be desired. Thomas R. Linden, Glaxo Wellcome Distinguished Professor of Medical Journalism and Mass Communication at the University of North Carolina at Chapel Hill bemoans the lack of good medical journalism on the web. He observes, "Compared to five years ago, when I wrote my guide to online medicine, there is much more health care material on the web. But it is harder now to find the good material and separate it from the bad." He attributes this to the fact that "Too many sites are too intent on promotion and fancy interactive tools, and they have lost site of good medical journalism".

So, while there is a need to consume health news on the World Wide Web and on the Internet with a very critical eye as to the source and reliability of the information and also the frequency with which it is updated, the benefits of online medical journalism also cannot be overlooked. In terms of the cheap health care it can offer, it opens up mind-boggling prospects of health care for those who cannot afford skyrocketing medical expenses. Unfortunately, at this juncture, visiting most medical sites is like tasting bad medicine because they are so boring, superficial and a waste of time. It requires experienced physicians to direct their patients to the better sites and steer them away from bad medicine and bad journalism.

But all is not lost. For the Internet is still a new medium and writers and website developers have to get used to it before they can use it optimally for e-medical journalism. So Linden offers advice on how it could be effectively utilized. He urges website developers to identify the author of any article that is more than a few paragraphs in length. He also wants the website to include the biographies of its authors and above all impresses upon the need for peer-review of 'every article with substantive medical content' by a medical expert.

The Medical Reporter/Editor/Reader Model

Like other forms of journalism, the process of medical journalism too is triune in character. At one end of its process is the medical reporter and at the other, the media audience. Mediating between the two is the medical editor. And, if we were to stretch the model a little further to keep in mind the economics of journalism, we could juxtapose the media proprietor with the editor. Also, passing through all these hands and virtually binding them to each other is the media message itself.

Medical Reporter

The editors of the New England Journal of Medicine noted recently that "the problem of communicating health is not in the research itself but in the way it is interpreted for the public. To facilitate the flow of pertinent medical research to public at large, we rely on the skills of medical journalists." (Scott Eggener, 1998)

The medical reporters occur in the beginning of the chain. It is they who hunt for the story, investigate it, pen it down and transmit it to the editor for his/her approval. In order that they might give a good account of themselves, it is necessary that they should be good not only at the general journalistic skills of digging out stories and reporting them but also at understanding the essentials of their stories. This implies that they should be well up in medical sciences. While it may not be necessary for them to be medicos, but it would certainly do them a world of good if they grounded themselves well in the basics of medical sciences. Otherwise, as the results of a recent survey show, they would find it difficult to measure up to the demands of their calling. The survey of medicos has revealed that in their opinion medical journalists "do an excellent job of reporting research only around 35 per cent of the time." This is so despite the fact that medical journalism is already being taught as a full fledged graduate programme in many US universities where training is imparted in areas as diverse as bio statistics, epidemiology, research methodologies and statistical analysis. It is for this reason that Jon Ziomek, Assistant Dean and Graduate Editorial Director at Northwestern University's Medill School of Journalism, emphasizes the need for 'connecting' classes in medical journalism with the broader, 'big picture' issues of science. Ziomek also wants that trainees must learn more about the business side of the health and medical industries. The universities delivering courses in medical journalism have found it useful to be linked up with other disciplines such as sociology, economics, history, political science, and social work and community development to examine these topics and give their students a wider view of the issues. A broad understanding of the mutual relationship between public policy, economics and medical science can enable them to write medical stories that highlight the role of the State and the market forces in doling out cheap and efficient medical care to the underdog in the society.

They should also master library research methods to quickly access multiple sources from respected research journals, the general and trade press. The uses of databases from online and compact disk material are essential, as is the knowledge of the Internet. They should be able to master the latest media interactive technologies and multimedia skills for combining text, audio, video and graphics as new career opportunities are opening up in the new media of cyberspace. While writing their stories, however, the medical journalists, must take care of the fundamentals such as: accuracy, validity, human context and appropriateness of information.

Editor

The editor occupies the middle ground between the medical reporter and the media audience. It is for him/her to assess the level, the quality and veracity of the medical reports/ stories submitted for publication. Also, it is for him/her to give the publication its singular identity in the market. To this end, (s)he has to utilize all the editorial skills at his/ her disposal.

Unfortunately, the stock of medical editing is still very low in most medical journals/magazines. It is for this reason that associations like World Association of Medical Editors (WAME) have come up on the horizon of medical journalism. In one of its recent reports, WAME observes: "Investigations of the quality of reports of health and medical research in medical journals and text books, and of the process of medical editing have revealed a variety of serious deficiencies and distortions, some of which pose indirect threats to the health of individuals and the wider public."

To salvage the situation, WAME has embarked upon a programme of training medical editors for their jobs, especially the ones who lack infrastructural support. Such an attempt should go a long way in boosting the standards of medical editing, as ignorance of medical editing is often the culprit in these cases. The reason being that most of the medical editors are basically medicos who have rarely ventured into the arena of medical journalism.

In discharging their duties, editors often have to contend with the interests of their masters – the media proprietors. And this is so not only when the proprietor is a business house/individual but also when the proprietor happens to be a professional organization. A case in point is that of the dismissal of the editor of the Journal of American Medical Association (JAMA), George Lunderberg by Surgeon E. Ratcliffe Anderson Jr., MD and CEO of American Medical Association. Lunderberg was fired apparently for publishing the results of a study on sex. The case made out was that he had unduly dragged an academic publication into political and racial controversy.

But deep down, it was otherwise. It was not the publication of the study that had violated the editorial code of conduct but the MD and CEO himself for he did so to appease a section of politicians who had disliked the study. So, it was the MD who had politicized the work of an editor.

Audiences

Unlike the audiences of other genres of journalism, the audience of medical journalism is divisible into two contrasting groups: while the first audience group has specialized knowledge of the subject-matter of medical journalism, the second audience group possesses at the best a generalist's knowledge of medicine and diseases. Again, the uses and gratifications that each wish to derive from it are also divergent. While the first group looks for the information advances in medicine and surgery that could enhance their professional efficiency and effectiveness, the second group seeks information on ways and means of curing ailments, either by oneself or with the help of professionals. So, while the demands of the first group are exacting and technical by scientific standards, those of the second group are simple and general.

Satisfying the needs of these two diametrically opposed audience groups, are the academic medical journals and general medical magazines or supplements/columns in popular media. Medical journals are written to give medics brief updates on the latest medical information. Medical journalists are needed to compile this information for doctors into stories that are accurate and brief, yet informative. As the end-users of these journals are specialists, the articles in these journals are often peer-reviewed before publication. However, not all medical journals for health care professionals are peer-reviewed which ultimately tells upon their quality. Medical magazines and supplements/columns in popular media, on the other hand, are meant to provide general medical information shorn of all medical jargon in an entertaining manner so that the largest number of readers gets hooked on to them. 'Medical Detectives' on Discovery Channel is an instance of medical journalism where the purpose is to arrest the attention of the viewers like any work of art would.

As the size of the second audience group continues to grow, medical stories in the popular media are bound to flourish. As per a recent survey carried out in Quebec, 44 per cent of the respondents were found to be aware of scientific issues, 70 per cent were not afraid of scientific and technical developments and only 36 per cent of the respondents believed that scientific progress would not improve the quality of life. The results clearly show that audiences have become scientifically minded. In such a media environment, medical journalism of the popular kind is bound to find a greater readership and viewership.

Media Message

What mediates between the medical reporter and editor, on the one end, and the audience, on the other, is the media message put out by the medical journalist. It is the quality of the message that determines the readership of a medical journal or article. This depends on the proper fusion of content and style. Emphasizing the need to marry the two, Christine German, Associate editor, *Time* advises: "Real classical literature to nurture good writing—ideas, images, metaphors — you have to keep constantly nourished in order to marry science and good writing together".

In fact, reporting through the experiences of people affected by the larger health issues, laced with analogy, metaphor and simile in a language people can understand is essential in medical journalism. In this section, we would like to discuss the various technical aspects of effective media message preparation.

Readable English

The editors of the biomedical journals must ensure that not only their own contributions in the form of editorials, commentaries and articles are of the highest standard in

English grammar, style and literature, but also that they insist on an equally high standard from their contributors. This can be achieved in various ways:

1. by rejecting outright and badly written papers.
2. by requesting badly written sections to be rewritten.
3. by making necessary corrections and improvements themselves where needed without reference to the contributors.

Commenting on the kind of language that medical journalists should use, Cathy Younger Lewis remarks that "if there's a simpler word, use it! And, further, watch how you read! When we're reading for pleasure, we don't want to expend too much energy. Allow your reader to use fewer neurons by writing simply and to the point".

Pictures

These play a major role in the effectiveness of health warnings. Warnings typically contain negative information (side effects) and this negative information is juxtaposed with positive (favourable) information or positive symbols (attractive images) about the product or service. The impact of pictorial warnings is illustrated in experiments in which respondents report dangers of products such as beer, ice cream and cigarettes. Pictorial and non-pictorial warnings were attached to advertisements for those products. Selection of warnings by manufacturers and service providers can and should be based on empirical demonstration of the efficacy of those warnings.

Cartoons

People are often reluctant to process health messages about life threatening illnesses because of fear. Often, the most fearful people are those who are the most at risk and thus the most in need of behaviour change. Studies are being conducted in the US to examine the use of cartoons as the means of preparing effective messages.

Evaluation of Medical Journalism

Having looked at the meaning, the forms and the process of medical journalism, we may now evaluate it with the yardstick of ethics. Ethically speaking, medical journalism performs the notable role of filling in the information gap between the professionals, who may be at times inaccessible to the ordinary man in the street and the info-hungry health/disease conscious media audience. Notwithstanding the disclaimer on most medical journals/articles, readers often look up to medical articles/journals for guidance concerning their ailments, which may sometimes be chronic. So, when they get any such information they immediately act upon it. This makes it obligatory on the part of the medical journalists to be exact in their coverage of medical/health issues. But the media house for which they work is not there for charitable purposes. It has its own profits to think about. And the barometer of profits rests more on the aesthetics than on grim truth, especially in the case of medical/health issues. Doing up of media message to increase its aesthetic appeal to the readers might entail sacrifice of vital information related to health care. And in many cases, it might entail distortion of information. According to a study made by Ray Moynihan, a journalist with *The Australian Financial Review* (results reported in *New England Journal of Medicine*), "there were too many breakthroughs, too many wonder drug stories, too many miracle cure stories... huge PR companies shamelessly using the media to promote their products, but not promote their products in advertising, promote their products in the editorial pages of the newspapers, or on ABC News, or on Channel Seven or Channel Nine...So I guess I identified a problem of too much journalism looking too much like promotion". Echoing his opinion, David Shaw writes in the *Los Angeles Times*, "It seems as if there are Page 1 stories, television news reports and magazine cover stories almost daily on medical breakthroughs". Shaw finds the process by which medical news is reported as 'severely flawed' and to "make matters worse, many medical stories are simply artful rewrites of press releases put out by profit minded medical journals'. Shaw also documents a case of *New York Times* article that seemed to predict an imminent cure for cancer.

Again, another problem impinging on ethics in medical journalism is the credentials of medical journalists themselves. When the American Medical Writers Association (AMWA) was founded in 1940, its membership consisted almost entirely of those with MD degrees. Over the next 50 years, however physician membership in AMWA steadily declined. In 1955, 76 per cent of members possessed a MD degree, yet in 1991 this figure dropped to 9 per cent. Betty Cohen, former president of AMWA, explains, "As AMWA evolved, other non physician writers entered, bringing different expertise. Physicians may have felt it was no longer their organization". Since 1991, this trend has begun to reverse itself and as AMWA membership has increased by 20 per cent to 4000 members, physicians now comprise 12.5 per cent of all members. There are few data available to assess the total number of physician writers without ties to professional organizations.

On the whole, it presents a grim scenario, as non-medicos writing for medical columns and journals cannot be expected to have the same level of insight into medical problems as medicos themselves would have. There can be serious errors also in reporting.

Conclusion

The preceding discussion of the meaning, forms, process and evaluation of medical journalism shows that medical journalism is here to stay and grow. As more and still more people grow health conscious, they are bound to turn to medical journals/columns in print, electronic and online media for help and advice. This will put a greater burden of responsibility on medical journalists in terms of the veracity of information they provide, if they are to uphold the ethics of their profession. As far as the economics of medical journalism are concerned, greater readership/

audiences implies greater circulation and greater advertisement support, as long as the media establishments maintain the integrity of their product-media information. Besides, phenomenal rise in health care costs due to the opening up of the health sector to market forces making medical care highly prohibitive for the common man is sure to help in the popularization of the cheaper alternative offered by medical journalism.

NOTES

1. Scott Eggener in 'The Power of the Pen: Medical Journalism and Public Awareness' (Pulse-Report, Vol. 279, p. 1400, May 6, 1998) observes:

   As long as a discrepancy exists between medical wisdom and the health of the population, there will be a valued role for the medical journalist.

   In support of his argument, he quotes David Satcher, MD, US Surgeon General who maintains:

   We have come to a point where, unless we can communicate to people outside of medicine, we can not achieve a lot of our goals.
2. The biomedical field is supposed to include 'the areas of medicine, health policy, pharmaceutics, communication, marketing, and electronic media.
3. *Meditrack* is a medical journal published from Ludhiana, Punjab on a monthly basis. It claims a wide readership among both the general public and the medicos.

REFERENCES

www.abc.net.au / rn / talks / 8.30 / mediarpt / stories / s136812.htm
www.ama.assn.org / sci-pbs / msjama / articles / vol279 / no.17
www.columbia.edu / cu / 21stc / issue-4.2 / skolmic / html
www.icdi.wvu.edu / diability / tables.html
www.ncbi.nlm.nih.gov / pubmed
nasw.org / users / bschachter / breakthrough.html
www.usc.edu / content / spike.cfm?request=291

13

MEDIA AND LITERACY MOVEMENT IN INDIA
Some Critical Issues

SURESH CHAND AND KULWINDER SINGH

Mass communication is a catalytic agent in the modernization process. There are several areas : increasing the flow of information, stimulating participation in development and making education more efficient or effective, where communication plays a significant role in accelerating the process of development. Education makes a significant contribution to national development through the development of a nation's human resources. An illiterate person has hundreds of enemy: epidemics, hunger, disorder and humiliation. Therefore, it is essential that illiteracy has to be eradicated. So, the National Literacy Mission (NLM) was set up by the Government of India in recognition of the need for priority attention to adult literacy for speeding up the development process and was launched by the Prime Minister of India on 5th May, 1988 to eliminate illiteracy by 1995 as a technical and societal mission.

National Policy on Education (1986) laid emphasis on adult and continuing education: *Both the literate and the educated will be sensitized to take literacy work with as sense of pride patriotism and social obligation. The community of learners will be motivated and mobilized for literacy to perceive the need for literacy and internalize this need for their collective well-being. For this purpose, environmental building activities would continue to be taken through organization of Jathas, street plays and nukad nataks, wall writings, literacy songs and slogans, articles in newspapers and magazines by creative writers, thinkers and opinion leaders etc.*

Further, it is laid down that media would be used in literacy promotion as a tool of dissemination of knowledge, as a tool of mobilization, motivation and sensitization, as a tool of learning by sharing information, ideas and experiences and as a tool of social action for change. For this purpose, discussion on various aspects relating to literacy would be arranged on Doordarshan and Radio, spots and motivational films would be produced and shown on TV and classes conducted through radio. Both print and non-print media, including traditional folk art would be fully harnessed for disseminating the message of literacy and for creating a positive climate for literacy.

The National Literacy Mission (NLM) established in 1988 adopted the environmental building programme in form of rallies, *Pad Yatras, Kala Jathas,* competition, discussion, and full utilization of print and visual media. The launching of special programmes for neo-literate adults, among rural women folk and news coverage of various programmes/initiatives taken up by voluntary organizations have been highlighted by the print media. However, with passage of time, the news coverage, advertisements and its off-spins has come to naught in media. The success of literacy movement during previous decade is reflected that India will attain the sustainable threshold of literacy (75%) by 2005-2006 as reported by NSSO survey (1997). It has to be made possible by concerted efforts by voluntary organizations in the spirit of mission mode and various literacy movement activities related with social, economic, cultural and political development.

The Joshi Committee points out that media can help in eradication of illiteracy

1. by neutralizing the resistance of the traditional intelligentia to mass literacy and education,
2. by winning ever and mobilizing the patriotic and idealistic elements among them as leaders of literacy and educational campaigns,

3. by neutralizing apathy and passivity of masses to the question of their literacy and education and making them aware of its importance in fighting the forces which keep them oppressed and poor, and
4. by consolidating the active and sensitive elements among the masses as leading forces for rousing the others from their apathy.

Various combinations of media have been used in the massive national adult education campaign in Cuba, China and Tanzania. There very large national campaigns make use of national political mobilization and feed the nation with information and material through a large number of channels. In Cuba, the literacy campaign of 1961 made use of all the secondary students and teachers in the nation to teach adults. The radio was filled daily with stories of achievement and success. The newspaper carried special pages written in large type-face for the neo-literate to read. Sets of posters were produced in mass quantities for display in adult education centres and meeting places. The result of the multiplicity of media involved and the support of the Government made the campaign a national movement.

In Functional Literacy Project in Tanzania a series of newspapers were started to remedy the situation of rarity of newspaper in rural areas. These papers contained news about events in nearby villages and people. Such newspapers were inexpensive. The language used is such that it does not go beyond the vocabulary of the neo-literates.

But in India various development processes which were due to the literacy movement have not attracted the desired attention of mass media. As envisaged in UNESCO report on various aspects of communication and society that *'dissemination of knowledge', 'socialization', 'motivation', 'promoting debate and discussion on public issues', 'education', 'cultural promotion', 'entertainment', and integration* are the functions of mass media. But main thrust of media is on entertainment, promotion of consumerism, negative aspects such as thrillers, suspense and orthodoxy etc., which is not in the direction of developing attributes and attitudes among people for their effective role in national development. In the field of education particularly in literacy movement media have not played active role which was expected from media. Success stories of innovations used by volunteers and NGO's, *Kala Jathas* who mobilized masses to participate in literacy movement has not highlighted by media. September 8th is observed as International Literacy Day projecting the importance of literacy. The print media as well as electronic media had a very limited coverage of International Literacy Day and its observance. Arvind Bhandari's article *'Depressing Performance on Literacy Front'* in *The Tribune* and *Dina Nath Mishr's Nirakcharta Ke Kalank Se Chutkare Ki Aas* in *Dainik Jagran* in September 2000.

Scanty coverage of news regarding various inputs in literacy, success stories of innovations used by volunteers and different non-governmental organizations is a reflection of apathy on the part of media.

Media policy is expected to play its role not only for awareness and inculcating pro-social and developmental values among illiterate masses for their movement towards literate world, but also to sensitize and activate the educated (privileged) people to contribute cause of mass educability. The beginning made by Doordarshan in the form of educational channel 'Gyan Darshan' is a welcome step, though it presently caters only to the educated sections.

But we cannot blame only media because there are numerous constraints such as structural, ideological, political, leadership, institutional permanency, finance, planning and management, content development, production, distribution and reception which hinder the realization of their potential.

The targeting of adult population's needs and aspirations is still to emerge as priority. Media is urban-biased, so media should highlight the problems of the rural people. Some programmes with a focus on illiterate and neo-literates masses may be telecast/broadcast for increasing awareness among people. Language of the programmes should be simple and timing of the programmes should be according to the needs of target population so that they reach the maximum population. National Literacy Mission needs to bring regular write-ups on the literacy in all newspaper by encouraging it through advertisements and other visual strategies.

All newspapers should cover such events focusing on role of literacy in development, health and hygiene and environmental awareness. Due coverage should be given to the news of seminars, symposia and functions of social organization aiming at welfare of the society. The development plans and other programmes should be covered adequately for proper dissemination of the message by the media users. Literate and educated persons can be motivated to teach the illiterates. The campaigns and mass movements can be built only if the media assumes a constructive approach. Further, the neo-literates, especially ruralites and women need support from print media for strengthening of literacy skills and their empowerment. Lastly, if media is to be for people, then the shift in media policy is to be regulated only in the essence of media's role as defined by various national and international commissions and committees for democratization of information, promoting development ethos among people for national development in the broad framework of changing international scenario.

REFERENCES

Acharya, R.N. *Television in India*. Delhi: Manas Publication, 1978.

Government of India. *National Policy on Education* 1986. New Delhi: MHRD, 1986.

Jamison, Dean T. and McAnany Emile G. *Radio for Education and Development*. Beverly Hills, Sage Publication, 1978.

Joshi, P.C. Television, Culture and Communication. *Mainstream*, June 4, 1983.

Singh, U.K. and Sudershan, K.N. *Media Education*, New Delhi: Discovery Publishing House, 1996.

Sodhi, T.S. *Adult Education: A Multidisciplinary Approach*.

14

MEDIA AND ENVIRONMENTAL AWARENESS

AMAR BHUSHAN AGGARWAL

Environmental pollution is enemy number one of today's materialistic society. The world is facing a serious challenge to save its environment from pollution as the very survival of life on this planet is threatened. All over the world increasing harm is being caused to the ecology and that people are not adequately motivated towards waging a collective war against the forces of environmental pollution. The developed countries are indeed the greatest polluters, who account for 70 per cent of the atmospheric pollution and the developing world is always at the receiving end has been helpless spectators. Pollution has been adversely affecting the atmosphere and the climate and thereby affecting the human society.

Before we talk of the role of media in combating environmental pollution, first of all we may study the various causes of pollution and efforts of government and NGO's put in to check pollution.

Urbanization, industrialization, exploding population, ever increasing number of vehicles and deforestation are some of the major causes of environmental pollution. As a result there are increasing number of diseases, global warming, depletion in ozone sphere and acid rains etc. Biological and ecological degradation has direct impact on the quality of life of living organisms and depletion of natural resources. Even rivers, streams and ponds have been polluted due to increasing use of insecticides, pesticides and nitrogenous fertilizers.

A recent study by the Centre for Science & Environment has revealed that Air Pollution in India has been killing nearly 52,000 people in 36 Indian cities every year prematurely while hospitalizing about 26 million. According to a study carried out by the National Environmental Engineering Research Institute in association with World Bank and Indira Gandhi Institute of Developmental Research (IGIDR) estimated the health costs due to air pollution in the NCT region of Delhi is about 117 crore per year and loss of vegetation costs about 32 crore during the same period.

Another study by the IGIDR, Mumbai states that out of the 23 major Indian cities, Delhi is the most air polluted city and is also one among the top ten most polluted cities in the world. It ranked fourth among the 41 cities of the world monitored for air pollution caused mainly by automobiles numbering 30 lakh. The vehicular pollution alone accounts for nearly 72 per cent of the total air pollution in India.

Many animal species in India have become extinct. The National Institute of Oceanography has reported that shrimp, prawn and fish yield off Kerala coast has declined by 25 per cent due to coastal pollution.

World's worst ecological disaster was created by the Gulf War which was almost equal to the combined disasters of Hiroshima, Bhopal and the Chernobyl.

Besides urbanization and industrialization, burning of fuel wood is another major source of air pollution in India. Large scale destruction of forest resources not only causes serious economical, social hazard and depletion of forest cover but at the same time causes increase in percentage of harmful gases like sulphur dioxide and monoxides and dioxides of carbon etc. resulting in acid rain, global warming and other such dreaded results.

The first world concern for environment can be traced to the United Nations Conference on Human Environment at Stockholm in June 1972. The Stockholm Conference not only marked the beginnings of environmental revaluation but it also signified media's commitment to the cause of environmental awareness and sustainable development.

In India, our environmental awareness can be traced to protests raised against setting up of a petroleum refinery at Mathura barely 40 kms from Agra which was a threat to our world famous historical monument—the Taj Mahal—which you all know very well. Sustained efforts through press, several societies and institutions including the prestigious Indian Heritage Society, the Bombay Natural History Society and the Archaeological Survey of India resulted in the government agreeing to shifting the refinery, closing down two thermal plants located at Agra and also shifting the existing small scale industries and foundries to an area beyond Taj apart from provision for establishing a green belt between Agra and Mathura.

The media also played a notable role in carrying forward the message of Chipko movement. The non-violent, action oriented Chipko movement attracted the attention of environmentalists, organizations interested in the process of social change and the media throughout the world.

Print media in India have also played a pivotal role in focussing attention of the people regarding the problems of environment. Several newspapers and magazines have started regular columns on subjects like ecology, environmental pollution, afforestation, wild life, conservation and development. Leading newspapers *The Times of India, The Hindustan Times, The Hindu, The Indian Express, The Statesman*, *The Tribune* have been regularly disseminating information about environmental issues. Magazines like *Yojna, Kurukshetra, Vidura, Down to Earth* etc. have been presenting thought provoking articles and reviews on the issues pertaining to environment. The Hindi language and regional press have also been highlighting environmental issues and guiding the people activities at the grassroot level.

Teleserials like 'Rakshak', 'Virasat', Our Inheritance, Cultural Heritage etc. have been useful sources of information and enlightenment to the audience. That apart, talks, interviews and panel discussions organised by Doordarshan have also been useful to audience to gain new insight and outlook in regard to environmental pollution. AIR has also been providing talks, discussions etc.

The efforts of NGO's, environmental groups, institutions like Centre for Science & Environment and individuals like Sunderlal Bahuguna, Medha Patkar, Anil Aggarwal, Vandana Shiva and journalists like Bharat Dogra have gone a long way in creating awareness about different aspects of environmental problems. Of late the judicial intervention at the highest level by the Supreme Court of India has also added to the consolidation of environmental movement.

The Supreme Court of India recently ordered a limit on the number of cars that may be registered monthly in Delhi. With the new Supreme Court ruling, this number has been limited to 1500 per month. And all vehicles must be compliant with specific exhaust emission standards. Previously over 4000 vehicles per month were being sold in Delhi.

With a view to create environmental awareness among various age groups and to disseminate information, priority has also been accorded to the areas of environmental education by the Ministry of Environment & Forests. Special emphasis is given to non-formal environmental education through seminars, symposia, workshops, training programmes, eco-camps, audio-visual shows etc. National environmental campaigns are also being organised by the Ministry since July 1986. A new scheme 'Paryavaran Vahini' has been launched since 1992-93 to create environmental awareness and to ensure active public participation by involving local people in the activities related to environmental protection.

'International Earth Summit' at Rio (Latin America) in June 1992 called for the introduction of the 'Polluter Pays Principle' to prevent global environment degradation. The United Nations Conference on Environment & Development estimated that 125 billion dollars should be given annually to the developing countries to pay for environmental protection plans but nothing has been done. The indifferent attitude of the developed countries including USA is the major hurdle towards any environmental protection programme at international level.

Inspite of a host of measures taken by the government institutes, NGO's and individuals in conserving environment, there does not seem to be any appreciable progress in preventing the rush of the nation towards ecological doomsday. In fact no environmental programme can be successful unless the support for the cause comes from below. Specially people living in close association with nature. For any such programme to be successful it is therefore very important to inculcate awareness among the masses. And this too should be done in a manner which can easily assimilate with not only the educated and affluent people in the urban areas but also among the illiterate downtrodden people living in the rural and forest areas.

Now the question is how to reach such masses spread over such a vast area segregated into a large number of culturally and linguistically different regions. To evolve any such channel catering to their need for environmental awareness would be a pipe dream for any government. It is here that the media—both print and electronic assume an important role. Though several audio-visual programmes are being organised by the government through the Directorate of Field Publicity or through the NGO's, the feasibility of the programme is limited in terms of the extent of their coverage. Hence the role of mass media for dissemination of environmental information among the masses spread throughout the country has been recognized as more factual than any other communication means. For sustaining development and creating environmental awareness, motivation and mobilization of people become essential and effective functions of the media.

A well planned strategy for creating environmental

awareness on the problems concerning degradation of environment and its impact on natural surroundings is vital. For this purpose, an appropriate media infrastructure covering environmental news in an intelligent manner is necessary. It is only the explosion of awareness on environmental concerns among the general public that can help the nation prevent the explosion of ecological imbalance.

The writers and reporters with in-depth knowledge and technical competence by circulating ideas concerning environmental problem in press may help in educating the people. Then the enlightened masses and NGO's may take up the task of spreading the message among the uneducated public through oral/inter-personal communication. It is high time when media should exploit all avenues to harness the energies of the common masses towards environmental protection.

To conclude I must say that environmental communication needs a priority based attention from the mass media. Though media cannot frame policies and make laws but it should help in building up a strong public opinion about this important discipline and transform it into a movement on the pattern of greenpeace movement of Europe.

15

ETHICAL DIMENSIONS IN INDIAN ADVERTISING

KISHORE C. RAUT

Advertising has become an integral part of our society. In a way, it has been deeply embedded in our daily lives. Its presence in every walk of life is so pervasive that it is almost impossible to escape the influence of advertising. Thus advertising of late has emerged as a forceful tool in moulding our attitudes and our behaviour towards products, services, images and ideas. It is a vital marketing tool as well as a powerful communication force. With the modern market glutted with endless brands in each category, the average consumer gets a freedom of choice in the market place. In the buyer's market, prospective buyers are largely influenced by advertising in their decision making process. Business for that matter too, lean heavily on advertising to survive in the ruthless competitive market. Business is viewed as a socio-economic institution rather than a strictly economic one. Business advertising as such need to be socially responsive to communicate to the prospective buyers about the products and services offered for sale by using various channels of information and persuade them to buy the same. In the process, such communication need to provide fair and truthful information.

Obviously, advertising and other marketing communications are attempts at persuasion besides providing information. Under normal conditions, such attempts of persuasion should not concern any one because the right to advocate one's position is essentially a privilege enjoyed by all in a free society. However, advertising often goes beyond their traditional role of providing *fair and truthful* information to the prospective buyers in making wise choices in the marketplace. However, there are instances galore where advertisements become brainwashing catalysts aiming at manipulating the buying decisions of the consumers in favour of products, services and ideas thereby invoking criticisms from the vanguards of social values. Deliberately or not, few advertisements move beyond the *'act of persuasion'* and 'provider of *truthful information*'. And, such manipulative aspect of advertising is socially detrimental since it challenges the prevailing value system and hence considered unethical.

Ethics : The Concept

Though there is no universally accepted definition of the word *"ethics'*. in common parlance, it is used to mean *right* or *wrong*. The Chamber's Dictionary defines ethics as 'the *science of morals* and that branch of philosophy which is concerned with human character and conduct'. Ethics is a choice between *good* and *bad,* between *right* and *wrong*. It is governed by a set of principles of morality at a given time in the society. The concept has some facets that are universal in nature, but much of it may be defined with reference to the values established and practised by a particular society. Thus, ethical conduct is not easy to understand and the determination of ethical conduct is subjective and vague, varying among different cultures, different religious groups and different sub-societal groups. Further, the concept of morality does not only differ in interpretation and application from culture to culture, but also witnesses change over a period of time even within the same culture. In the present context of growing liberalisation and globalisation in India, ethics has to be a part of economic success and not to be sacrificed because of it.

Ethical Values in Advertising

Advertising too has ethical values. Advertising as a popular form of communication is a mix of art and facts subservient to ethical principles and standards. In order to be pragmatically consumeristic, advertisements necessarily have to be truthful and ethical. It should, under no circumstances, mislead, misinform and misguide the consumers. Normally the purpose of advertising should be to inform, persuade in conformity with the prevailing ethical standards that draw their roots from the social norms and values, ultimately reinforcing the social value orders. And, any deviation from this without substantive justifiabilities would be viewed as an affront to the tradition, moral and ethically bound society. If that happens, the credibility of advertising is simply lost. As far as ethical values in advertising are concerned, the concept of *right* and *wrong*, *fair* and *unfair*, *just* and *unjust* is reflected either by the organisational policy or by social reactions to a given advertisement.

Ethical Dilemmas in Advertising

An objective analysis and assessment of an advertisement sometimes, becomes improbable since many a time a clear line of demarcation between what is true and what is untrue is really difficult to establish. One of the peculiar aspects that confront the ethical norms in advertising is that any advertisement as such is judged by its impact and by its acceptance by the consumers at large. As a matter of fact, it is often argued that if the objective of advertising is to change the personal traits of the consumers and effect the desired buying behaviour, the very objective of advertising can be questioned on the grounds of manipulativeness. In other words, any advertising which aims at persuading people and attempts to mould or reinforce their behaviour in favour of products, services, images and ideas, as such need some manipulative tactics and hence can be considered unethical. However, in reality, there is hardly any advertisement, which would not attract the flaks of the moral police if the concept of ethics is strictly adhered to. For that reason, advertising has often been called the *"permissible lie'.*

In a modern economy, dependence by business on advertising for survival in a highly competitive market is a forgone conclusion.

In such a case, every single advertisement undertaken by the business world would be found napping; more or less violating the ethical norms of the society. Therefore if the objective of advertising is simply to inform people about the quality of products, services or ideas and provide them the freedom of choice, maintenance of ethical standard is possible. But once it goes beyond from 'providing information' to 'persuading to buy', small doses of manipulative tactics are needed to achieve such an objective. In all such cases, emphasis on psychological benefits, slightly exaggerated claims or even a small pinch of puffery are accepted by the society and can be considered ethical. That is why products/services advertised as 'best' or 'most often used', 'mostly recommended by doctors' or 'long lasting', etc. are even morally acceptable. In such cases, the demarcation is based on the *relativity of ethics* rather than *the ethical absolutism.* However, advertising that move beyond the socially permissible norms of manipulation and persuasion, would be considered unethical.

Critics firmly believe that advertisers make every effort in studying the intricacies of human mind in order to understand where the individual vulnerabilities lie. It is one of these vulnerabilities that they play to make the consumer feel that the redemption of the same lies in the possession or use of a particular product or service. This principle is being used by the advertisers in a very subtle manner and they hit where it hits the most and this led to their being labelled as *'the mind manipulators'* or *'the hidden persuaders'.* Indeed, many publications and research studies on advertising and its impact have focussed on the manipulative strategies adopted by the advertising world. Needless to say that, many of the methods employed by the advertisers to consumers can be considered 'unethical'.

As opposed to such blatant criticisms, advertising has many votaries who consider it an ideal medium for modern day communication. Supporters of advertising feel that advertising alone cannot be blamed for trends such as the level and nature of consumption in the society. They argue that advertising merely offers information about available choices to help consumers satisfy their own perceived needs. In a nutshell, they believe that the consumers as such exercise a rational choice and advertisers are not powerful enough to intervene in that process. Proponents point out that advertising and consumerism are natural allies and go hand in hand. In this scheme of things, it is the role of advertising to take consumers from an ill-informed wilderness into the real world of commodities. As it does this, it also provides the necessary impetus to keep the market buoyant, helping to maintain a high level of production and affluence.

'Ethics' as we have understood is the set of principles that distinguishes good from bad and has its connotations in the social value system, idealism, morality, decency, etc. Ethics should reflect not only in own perceptible thought process but also in our actions—individual, group or social. The various aspects of ethics range from the validity claims made in advertisements to their mode of presentation. However, instead of embracing the whole gamut of ethical related (read *unethical !)* issues of advertising, the present paper attempts to sharp-focus few of the ethical dimensions of Indian advertising. In the process, the ethical debate concerning exploitation of religious sentiments, encouragement of self-medication, endorsement of products by children and sexual overtones in various commercial advertisements receives a close examination in the following paragraphs.

Exploitation of Religious Sentiments

Since times immemorial religion and commerce have been in harmony with each other in every society, India being no exception. References and inspirations from religion of course have been always with respect and discretion. Since religion is deep rooted in the Indian psyche, it most often finds expression in popular culture whether in folk art, painting, T-shirts or advertisements. Disquietingly, in recent years everything including religions are increasingly becoming a part of commerce in the consumerist Indian society. Few advertisements are guilty of abusing the cultural ethos and values of Indian society. Some advertisements not only pose serious challenges to the ageless Indian culture and ethos but adopt all possible means to exploit the religious sentiments of the consumers. In the print advertisement campaign of a television company Goddess Durga is portrayed carrying the different models of television in each of her ten hands instead of carrying weapons. And such an advertisement is inserted during the Puja festival intentionally when Goddess Durga is worshipped. Above all, the caption goes: *An Offer So Irresistible, No One Can Keep Their Hands Off Our TVs* (not even Goddess Durga!) such a copy is a clear case of exploiting the religious faiths of the Indian consumers with a Hindu majority population. Even Goddess Durga is made to endorse products by the commercial advertisers, posing a serious threat to the prevalent cultural value of the society. Some years back, an MNC had introduced a range of shoes in the Middle East with the calligraphy of Allah stamped on them. There was such an uproar in the Islamic world that the company was forced to withdraw the shoe range with public apology. Such attempts to play on the religious sentiments and emotions of the public for commercial mileage are nothing but unethical.

Encouragement of Self-Medication

Many advertisements often lure consumers to try a brand of medicine. However, between a consumer and the drug stands a chit of paper; namely a prescription. Advertising prompt consumers to ignore the prescription. Medicines often have toxicity and when taken in wrong doses for wrong reasons may aggravate a disease or trigger new complications. Yet one sees legions of medicine advertisements prompting people to take just one or two of a certain kind of medicine for faster, long-lasting relief (Exhibit - II & III). Medicines, whether of herbal or chemical origin, can produce side effects. Lured by the promise of immediate relief, patients often use drugs which results in symptomatic relief only.

The persistent advertisements of drugs extolling its virtues sans a single word about its possible side effects, encourages the habit of self-medication which is potentially dangerous. It is ironic that advertisements of cigarettes and *pan-masalas* carry statutory warnings but the numerous aurvedic, herbal or allopathic drugs are advertised in different media and sold without a word of caution. Thus it is really unethical to have advertisements of medicines which prescribe a dose of promise relief within a set time. The Drugs and Magic Remedies Act, 1954 has provisions to protect the public from objectionable advertisements. However, most of the medicinal advertisements are undertaken in the guise of consumer goods advertisements and hence escape the ethical check-gates.

Endorsement by Children

A lot many advertisements that appear in different media project children to be in need of the advertised product or endorse products and services so that parents are persuaded by their children to buy the same. Classical examples of such persuasive advertisements in recent times are 'Just Two Minutes Maggie Noodles' and 'I Love You Rasna'. While it is quite pleasing to see children appearing in advertisements, how ethical is it to make them recommend or endorse products and services especially those not directly meant for them?

Children tend to believe anything which is portrayed convincingly (read tactfully). Therefore advertisements featuring children are received positively by the younger generation, since children tend to emulate the child in the advertisement. As a matter of fact, children are the most vulnerable victims of catchy advertisements. Moreover, certain products primarily meant for children contain certain harmful elements. The notable ones being nickel in chocolates, brominated vegetable oils in soft drinks, fluoride in toothpaste, monosodium glutamate in certain noodles, and so on. Since they are not matured and lack the ability to differentiate between the truth and a lie, it is really unethical to portray children to endorse products, service and ideas.

Many countries in the West have banned using children endorsing products and services on the grounds of the morality. However, our country is yet to enact legislation so as to prohibit children from appearing in advertisements and endorsing the use of products and services.

Obscenity and Sexual Overtone

In recent years, there is a growing concern among different sections of the society regarding increasing obscenity and vulgarity contents in advertisements. It is observed that obscenity and sex appeals are no more subtle. Rather sex appeals are quite suggestive both in language and visuals in many advertisements which are bad in taste. Few years ago, the MR Coffee and Tuff Shoes advertisements had kicked up much dust inviting loudest protest from many quarters. Given the social fabric and cultural mores of the Indian society, most of the advertisements and their portrayal of women are bad in taste. The beauty of women have been abusively used by the advertisements—glib men to sell anything—be it a soap, towel, detergent, computer or even an automobile. As a matter of fact, the use of female anatomy in advertisements is widely visible in the globalised India. No doubt, sex has always been the essence of advertising and to explore the sensuality angle of women has attracted advertisers for centuries. Few advertisements, however, cross the boundaries of morality and decency and make use of erotica and obscenity in order to attract the immediate attention of the public. Similar also is the case of men whose masculinity and machoness are displayed in titillating manner in various advertisements so as to achieve greater mileage in marketing objective. Such a phenomenon is observed more particularly with MNCs who adopt a global strategy for marketing their products and, therefore, run advertisements which uses symbols and imagery of the west, in congruent of our own moral and ethical norms. Such advertisements are basically guilty of downgrading moral standards of our society and considered unethical.

Conclusion

As advertising is a social process, it must honour time tested norms of social behaviour and should not affront our moral sense. In a country like India where consumerism, born out of liberalization and globalization, is fast emerging as a major force, there is a strong case for social intervention in the matter of advertisements in order to ensure that they meet specific standards of truth and prevalent values of the society and do not violate ethical norms. True, mass media advertising is the only viable and economic way of providing marketing information to India's enormous population spread as it is, over a vast geographic terrain. While the argument that consumers in India at large need information is a familiar one, the fact remains that little advertising is purely informative. Most of the advertisements traverse beyond true and informative level, use questionable means and consumers at large are being willy-nilly goaded into life styles determined by the market forces. As a matter of fact, most of the commercial advertisements undertaken in India blatantly try to sell a handful of dreams invested in material products and push the consumers to the pinnacle of consumerism; buy it, buy now and buy more. In the cult of hardsell, only the virtues of the product are emphasized and the faults, if any, are not mentioned. However, flagrant abuse of all norms of decency and ethics standards by the advertisers in order to win consumers need to be curbed at any cost in order to safeguard the interests of our unsuspecting citizens.

Societies generally assert that advertising should be truthful and there are legal provisions, which attempt to make advertisements generally meet specific standards of truth. Certain agencies like the Advertising Agencies Association of India (AAAI) and the Advertising Standards Council of India (ASCI) also provide a regulatory framework for advertising. In the absence of any clear standard of approved ethical norms, it is left to the advertisers to adhere to their own personal standards. In recent years, the stress in advertising has shifted from technical features of the product to direct emotional appeal thereby creating enormous scope for the advertisers to violate the ethical norms. The aforesaid is a clear pointer that there are indeed a great deal of difference what the advertisers call *information and persuasion* and what many people see as *manipulation, distortion, confusion and exploitation of consumers.* In such a situation, self-policing by the advertisers is of crucial significance.

16

LANGUAGE PRESS IN INDIA : A Case Study of Oriya Newspapers

SUNIL K. BEHERA

Multi-ethnicity, multi-culture and multi-language are the hallmark of India. In fact, the country is any linguist's delight. The Indian Constitution has recognised 18 major languages but there are 1652 languages and dialects spoken as mother tongues by the people of India. With this backdrop, it becomes imperative and an attempt has been made to study the Indian Press and more particularly the language press. The mosaic of the Indian Press is made up of two distinct systems – the Indian language press system and the English press system. Though both the systems evolved during the colonial period their growth pattern was not uniform. While the English press grew faster with an educated elite as its audience, the Indian language press had a retarded growth due to lack of resources and lack of encouragement from the government. In spite of these odds it played a key role in India's struggle for independence. In free India, the language press found a better climate for its growth. The re-organisation of the States on linguistic basis and the subsequent development of the languages gave impetus to the sluggish language press system. As a result the language press today has established an edge over the once mighty English press.

The superiority of the Indian language press system becomes evident from the fact that at the end of 1998, the 18 principal Indian languages together accounted for 85 per cent of the total number of newspapers and 75 per cent of total circulation of the press in India.

The Hindi press a constituent of the Indian language

press system, tops both in number as well as in circulation. By the end of 1998, there were 17,836 Hindi newspapers constituting 41 per cent of the total newspapers published in India. The English newspapers' position was second with 6,517 publications. In circulation too, the Hindi press was in the lead, followed by the English press. In terms of circulation, *Anand Bazar Patrika*, a single edition Bengali daily from Calcutta tops the list with 5,86,637 copies whereas *The Times of India* having six edition in English with a circulation of 13,90,827 copies occupied first position among multi-edition dailies during 1998. The Malayalam, Bengali, Telugu, Kannada, Marathi, Gujarati and Punjabi press also had circulations to reckon with.

The Oriya press though not in the top bracket, yet maintains a unique position in terms of its coverage, content and also its qualitative improvements in printing. Another notable feature of the Oriya press is that, recently a number of mofussil newspapers invariably small ones with circulations ranging between a few hundreds to some thousands are published. This chapter is an attempt to highlight the salient features of Oriya language press, particularly Oriya dailies, pertaining to their growth, development, status and news programming practices.

Origin and Growth

Orissa or Odisha is in the mid-eastern region of the country surrounded by the border States of Andhra Pradesh in south, Madhya Pradesh in west, Bihar and West Bengal in north and the Bay of Bengal in east. Orissa was earlier known as Kalinga/Utkal. The principal language of the State, Oriya is believed to have been evolved between the third and eighth century A.D. Some scholars assert that Oriya language evolved from Dravidian language to which were later added Sanskrit and Pali. Thus the combination of Dravidian and Aryan languages brought about Oudri Prakruti or Oriya language. Bharat Muni's *Natya Shastra* mentions Oriya as Bibhasa or mixed language. Others feel that Oriya alongwith Bengali and Assamiya has evolved from *Magadhi*, the language of Magadh area, now known as Bihar. In the thirteenth century Oriya language began taking modern shape and Oriya literature of the fourteenth century flourished with epics like *Mahabharat* by Sarala Das. The sixteenth century gave birth to a host of Oriya writers like Kabi Samrat Upendra Bhanja and Kabisurya Baladev Rath whose writings are still very popular. Modern writing influenced by the west began in 19th century with writers like Radhanath Ray and Fakir Mohan Senapati.

Missionaries and the Oriya Press

The enormous contribution of Christian missionaries to print journalism in India is well known. After the British took over Orissa in 1803, the Christian missionaries came to Orissa in 1822. Rev. Charles Lacey established the first printing press in Orissa known as Orissa Mission Press in 1836 and edited and published the first non-government monthly newspaper in Oriya – the *Jnanaruna* in 1849. Rev. Charles Lacey also published *Utkal Government Gazette* in 1851 and *Prabodh Chandrika* in 1856. However, the birth of *Utkala Deepika*, a weekly journal in 1866 was a landmark in the history of Oriya journalism. The *Deepika* continued its publication for 71 years and fought righteously for the formation of a separate province of Orissa. Few publications like *Utkala Deepika, Sambad Bahika* and *Sambalpur Hiteishini* helped considerably in the promotion of Oriya literature and Oriya journalism.

The 20th century saw the emergence of weekly and daily newspapers and Oriya *Asha* the first Oriya newspaper was published by Sashi Bhusan Rath as a weekly in 1913. The weekly was later turned into a daily newspaper. The modern journalism in Orissa had its beginning with the establishment of *Samaj,* a People's Society publication by Pandit Gopabandhu Das in 1919. Later it was managed and edited by the veteran journalist Radhanath Rath. The paper still occupies top position in Oriya language journalism with the highest circulation and readership in the State. Then came, *Prajatantra*, an Oriya newspaper established by Harekrushna Mahatab, former Chief Minister of Orissa. The 70's witnessed the publication of *Dharitri*, another daily newspaper by yet another former Chief Minister, Mrs. Nandini Satapathy and his politician husband, Sri Debendra Satapathy. Over the years *Dharitri* has acquired the status of the second largest circulated newspaper of Orissa. However, *Sambad*, a technically sound newspaper, started in 1982 by Sri Soumya Ranjan Patnaik, the son-in-law of the longest serving Chief Minister of Orissa, Sri Janaki Ballav Patnaik claims (unconfirmed) to have the highest circulation in the State. *Sambad* is the only newspaper in the State of Orissa to be published simultaneously from Bhubaneswar, Cuttack, Berhampur, Rourkela and Balasore. A recent addition to the colour daily newspaper scene of Orissa is the *Samaya*, again published by Sri Ranjib Biswal, former Member of Parliament and son of Sri Basanta Kumar Biswal, a political heavy weight in the State of Orissa.

A closer examination of the establishment and ownership pattern of these Oriya language daily newspaper reveals that almost all the important newspapers of the State have been established under the ownership/editorship/ patronage of the VIP politicians of the State irrespective of their party affiliations. The Oriya dailies do perform their duties as the purveyor and carrier of political, economic and social news but when the need arises, these newspapers act as the mouth piece of their politician owners or patrons. Discerning these facts, it is a matter of great pride for a poverty stricken State like Orissa that these newspapers have grown in stature over the years and the State has also witnessed the publication of a number of mofussil/small newspapers catering to the local needs of the various regions of the State.

With the increase in literacy and the growth of the socio-economic conditions of the middle class, the press in Orissa has experienced enormous gains, both in number and circulation. Though Doordarshan and other cable TV channels command a good viewership, still a majority of the population depends on the press for detail news and information. The growing number of Oriya newspapers and their increase circulation and readership figures bear ample testimony to the fact of an upsurge in Oriya literature and journalism.

The Oriya press is dominated by *Samaj, Sambad, Dharitri, Prajatantra* and *Samay*—the big five dailies. Together they account for over 80 per cent of the total circulation of the dailies. On the whole, the Oriya press today presents a diverse and impressive picture in terms of their growth in numbers over the years. At the end of 1998, there were 655 Oriya newspapers consisting of 68 dailies, 2 bi/tri-weeklies, 132 weeklies, 81 fortnightlies, 260 monthlies, 85 quarterlies and 27 other periodicals as against 448 newspapers in 1993.

The Study

The present study was taken up on sample Oriya newspapers with specific objectives to find out –

1. the news-to-advertisement ratio in Oriya dailies.
2. the topics that dominate the newshole.
3. the importance given to local, regional, national and international news event and issues.

With these specific objectives, a content analysis of five leading Oriya dailies — *Samaj, Sambad, Dharitri, Prajatantra* and *Samay* was carried out based on a two-week sample drawn from the period June-August, 2000. Twelve issues of each sampled daily were analysed. The sampled issues were of one continuous week commencing from July 10, 2000 and one composite week constructed by choosing one week day in turn every two weeks beginning June 5, 2000. Sunday issues were excluded because on these days newspapers are programmed with more non-news items such as short stories, poems, literary criticism, philosophical and religious dissertations, film/theatre reviews etc.

Every news and advertisement item measured in column centimetre scale was considered as a unit of analysis. The headline, body copy and pictures were treated as an integral part of a news item. Pictures appearing without news stories such as cartoons, photo features, etc. were placed under 'other category'. Supplementary pages of all the sampled newspapers were not considered for analysis, while their regular features, articles and letters on the editorial pages were considered for the study.

Findings and Discussion

Table 16.1 to 16.4 are offered to describe the quantitative analysis of the various items that had appeared in the newspapers under study. The study showed that the sampled dailies as a whole devoted nearly 65.9 percent of their space to news and 34.1 per cent to advertisements. Table 16.1 shows that *Prajatantra* reported the highest percentage of news (74.39) followed by *Samay* (72.10) whereas *Dharitri* devoted the highest percentage of space to advertisements (39.03) followed by *Samaj* (37.75). [see Table 16.1 for details].

TABLE 16.1 : Distribution of Space between News and Advertisement

Dailies	*News space in col. cm*	*Advertisement space in col. cm*	*Total space*
Samaj	37,292	22,612	59,904
	(62.25)	(37.75)	(100)
Sambad	25,066	14,870	39,936
	(62.76)	(37.24)	(100)
Dharitri	30,436	19,484	49,920
	(60.07)	(39.03)	(100)
Prajatantra	29,708	10,228	39,936
	(74.39)	(25.61)	(100)
Samay	28,790	11,146	39,936
	(72.10)	(27.90)	(100)
Total	1,51,292	78,340	2,29,632
	(65.9)	(34.1)	(100)

Note : All figures in parentheses represent percentages.

As can be seen from Table 16.2 about 80 per cent of the newshole of the dailies belonged to hard/straight news-matter of fact reporting of events/issues, investigative and interpretative reports. *Samaj* devoted 86.9 per cent of its news space to straight news followed by *Dharitri* with 82 per cent. Features and articles took the second largest share of the newshole followed by editorials and letters. *Prajatantra* devoted the highest space of 14.46 per cent to the features and articles while *Samaj* devoted the least percentage of space (5.69). Editorials' share of space in newshole varied between 4.64 per cent in *Dharitri* and 6.17 per cent in *Sambad* (see Table 16.2 for details).

TABLE 16.2 Distribution of News hole (content type)

(in per cent)

Content type	*Samaj*	*Sambad*	*Dharitri*	*Prajatantra*	*Samay*
Straight news	86.90	79.50	82.00	76.79	81.65
Features/Articles	5.69	10.62	11.42	14.46	9.73
Editorials	5.08	6.17	4.64	5.28	5.94
Letters	1.72	2.38	0.78	2.94	1.68
Others	0.61	1.33	1.16	0.53	1.00
Total	100	100	100	100	100
	N=37,292 col.cm	N=25,066 col.cm	N=30,436 col.cm	N=29,708 col.cm	N=28,790 col.cm

With regard to news topics, the study showed that all dailies except *Prajatantra* provide prime importance to a political stories which make up the largest chunk of their newshole. Crime took the largest newshole space (10.56 per cent) in *Prajatantra*. As can be seen in Table 16.3, the largest space given to politics was by *Sambad* (14.10 per cent) followed by *Samay* (13.62 per cent). Stories about corruption charges/ scandals/enquiries had second position in all the dailies except *Dharitri* which gave second importance to news about crime. In all other dailies crime took the third place except *Prajatantra* in which politics secured the third position. All the newspapers under study devoted about 6 per cent of the newshole to sports stories followed by stories about economic/finance, government and accidents/natural disaster. Table 16.3 further indicates that

Samaj gave the preferential allocation of space in the prioritised order to politics, corruption, crime, sports, economic/finance, reporting of problems, irregularities and complaints, accidents and natural disaster and so on. Almost the same sequence is followed by all the other newspapers with little variations as mentioned earlier.

TABLE 16.3 Distribution of Newshole (Topic Categories)

(in per cent)

Content type	*Samaj*	*Sambad*	*Dharitri*	*Prajatantra*	*Samay*
Politics	12.9	14.10	11.60	9.75	13.62
Crime	8.36	8.69	9.45	10.56	8.74
Human Interest	2.42	3.45	5.28	4.28	5.02
Sports	5.94	6.10	6.08	5.30	5.72
Defence/ National Security	0.88	0.32	1.06	1.24	0.78
Economic/ Finance	5.38	4.74	8.42	7.28	4.93
Accident/ National Disaster	4.65	5.22	3.74	4.11	5.09
Birth/death	3.52	1.46	2.80	1.15	2.30
Environment/ Natural Resources	2.80	2.24	2.64	2.34	1.96
Education	2.45	1.96	0.42	1.90	0.82
Foreign Affairs	2.21	2.00	2.18	2.42	2.60
Judiciary (Court/Law and Order)	3.72	3.20	2.68	2.36	3.34
Government	4.51	5.48	6.26	7.42	5.82
Science and Technology	1.92	0.74	2.30	1.52	0.46
Weather	1.39	1.02	1.82	1.24	1.18
Agriculture/ Food	2.64	1.48	1.22	1.38	2.20
Region	0.84	0.14	0.00	0.62	0.34
Art and Culture	2.69	2.32	1.88	2.42	1.09
Youth/ Women affairs	3.80	3.74	4.64	3.18	2.66
Problems/ irregularities/ complaints	4.68	4.04	4.32	5.13	5.32

TABLE 16.3 (*contd.*)

Content type	*Samaj*	*Sambad*	*Dharitri*	*Prajatantra*	*Samay*
Health/ Family Welfare	1.52	1.96	2.30	1.46	1.93
Parliament/ Assembly	1.00	1.84	3.68	3.20	2.08
Travel/ Tourism	3.12	2.84	1.96	1.48	2.13
Information/ Mass Media	1.64	1.98	0.83	1.21	1.42
Strikes/ Protests/ Hartals	2.20	4.69	2.76	3.10	4.08
Corruption charges/ Scandals/ Enquiries	8.76	11.42	8.98	10.24	12.10
Others	4.06	2.83	0.70	3.71	2.27
Total	100 N=37,292 col.cm	100 N=25,066 col.cm	100 N=30,436 col.cm	100 N=29,708 col.cm	100 N=28,790 col.cm

Table 16.4 clearly explains the region-wise distribution of news in the sampled newspapers. The reading material was not on far and distant environs, but on the immediate surrounding of the readers. The analysis showed that Oriya dailies are attuned to their own region. It becomes evident from Table 16.4, that they devote the largest space to regional news, that is news relevant to Orissa originating from within and outside the State. About 52 per cent of the space was devoted to regional news by all the newspapers. The national news had the second largest coverage in all the newspapers except *Sambad* which gave the second largest coverage to local news. *Samaj* tops the national news coverage with 23.62 per cent as against 20.68 per cent in *Dharitri,* 19.65 per cent in *Prajatantra*, 19.6 per cent in *Samay* and 18.1 per cent in *Sambad*. The multi-edition daily, *Sambad* devoted more space to local news — news relevant to the edition local circulation zone (21.32 per cent). Local news secured third place in all other newspapers except *Samaj.* As regards international news,

Samaj tops the chart with 12.36 per cent followed by *Samay* (10.12 percent), *Dharitri* (9.78 per cent), *Sambad* (8.85 percent) and *Prajatantra* (7.35 per cent).

TABLE 16.4 Distribution of Newshole (Region-wise)

(in per cent)

Content type	*Samaj*	*Sambad*	*Dharitri*	*Prajatantra*	*Samay*
Local News	10.21	21.32	14.64	16.94	15.70
Regional News	52.46	49.82	53.36	52.30	51.84
National News	23.62	18.10	20.68	19.65	19.60
International News	12.36	8.85	9.78	7.35	10.12
Others	1.35	1.91	1.54	3.76	2.74
Total	100	100	100	100	100
	N=37,292 col.cm	N=25,066 col.cm	N=30,436 col.cm	N=29,708 col.cm	N=28,790 col.cm

The pre-occupation of Oriya dailies with regional/ national issues, events and people is not a new trend and this practice continues since long—may be because of the non-publication of many English newspapers in the State. At present only two editions of *The Indian Express* and *The Asian Age*, are being published from Bhubaneswar, the capital city of Orissa. Thus, such news practices of giving priority to regional news followed by national instead of local is understandable in the absence of a well developed English press in the State.

Conclusion

The Oriya press at the best functions as informer and interpreter in the Orissan society. The link between growth of Oriya press and urbanization, industrialization, income and rise in literacy hints at the trend that information and communication process in the State of Orissa has supported to a large extent, the development process and vice-versa. The Oriya press, though politically affiliated and owned, has acted as a social monitor, constructive critic, stimulator of debates on public issues and as a moulder of public opinion. With the exception of few, the Oriya press in general swing in tune with public opinion lending ready support to popular public demands, be it social or political.

With the constant increase in literacy and the reader oriented editorial policies, the Oriya press as a whole registers growth and the press makes substantial changes for technical and editorial excellence even in the face of growing competition from the electronic media. At this pace, however, it has a long way to go.

LIST OF PARTICIPANTS

1. Sh. Shyam Khosla,
   President, NUJ & Veteran Journalist,
   New Delhi
2. Sh. Radhye Shyam Sharma,
   Editorial Advisor,
   Dainik Bhaskar,
   Chandigarh
3. Sh. Prem Kumar,
   Ex-Editor, Indian Express,
   Chandigarh
   (National Media Centre, Gurgaon)
4. Prof. M.R. Dua,
   Ex-Professor IIMC, New Delhi
   (National Media Centre, Gurgaon)
5. Prof. Vepa Rao,
   Department of Journalism and
   Mass Communication,
   H.P. University, Shimla
6. Prof. B.K. Kuthiala,
   Chairman, Department of Communication
   Management and Technology,
   GJU, Hissar
7. Ravi Kumar Dhar,
   Associate Professor,
   Department of Journalism & Languages,
   Punjab Agricultural University, Ludhiana

8. Dr. R.S. Dalal,
   Associate Prof., Extension Education
   Secretary to Vice-Chancellor,
   Haryana Agricultural University,
   Hissar
9. Dr. M.M. Goel,
   Former Chairman,
   Department of Journalism,
   Kurukshetra University, Kurukshetra
10. Dr. Sanjeev Bhanawat,
    Head, Department of Journalism,
    Rajasthan University,
    Jaipur
11. Dr. Sunil Behera,
    Head, Department of Journalism and
    Mass Communication,
    Berhampur University,
    Berhampur (Orissa)
12. Dr. Saroj Dahiya,
    Professor,
    College of Home Science,
    CCS Haryana Agricultural University,
    Hissar
13. Ms. Shital Thapar,
    Asstt. Professor,
    Department of Journalism & Languages,
    Punjab Agricultural University, Ludhiana
14. Prof. J. P. Bhati,
    Professor of Economics & Director,
    Population Research Centre,
    H.P. University, Shimla
15. Dr. Kulwinder Singh,
    Department of Education,
    H.P. University, Shimla
16. Mr. Suresh Chand,
    Department of Education,
    H.P. University, Shimla

17. Mrs. Manju Lohumi,
    ICDEOL,
    H.P. University, Shimla
18. Ms. Nisha Sharma,
    Research Scholar, Department of Education
    HPU, Shimla
19. Prof. Jaishri Jethwani,
    Professor, Indian Institute of
    Mass Communication,
    New Delhi.
20. Prof. V.S. Gupta,
    Ex-Prof., Haryana Agricultural
    University, and former Country
    Representative, AMIC, Singapore,
    Vasant Kunj, New Delhi.
21. Dr. Kishore Raut,
    Reader in Commerce,
    Marketing & Advertising
    Berhampur University, Berhampur
22. Sh. A.B. Aggarwal,
    Freelance Writer, Patiala
23. Dr. T.D.S. Alok,
    Reader, Department of Journalism and
    Mass Communication,
    H.P. University, Shimla
24. Dr. Harish,
    Reader, Department of Journalism and
    Mass Communication,
    Rohtak University, Rohtak
25. Dr. (Mrs.) Vir Bala Aggarwal,
    Chairperson, Department of Journalism and
    Mass Communication
    H.P. University, Shimla

INDEX